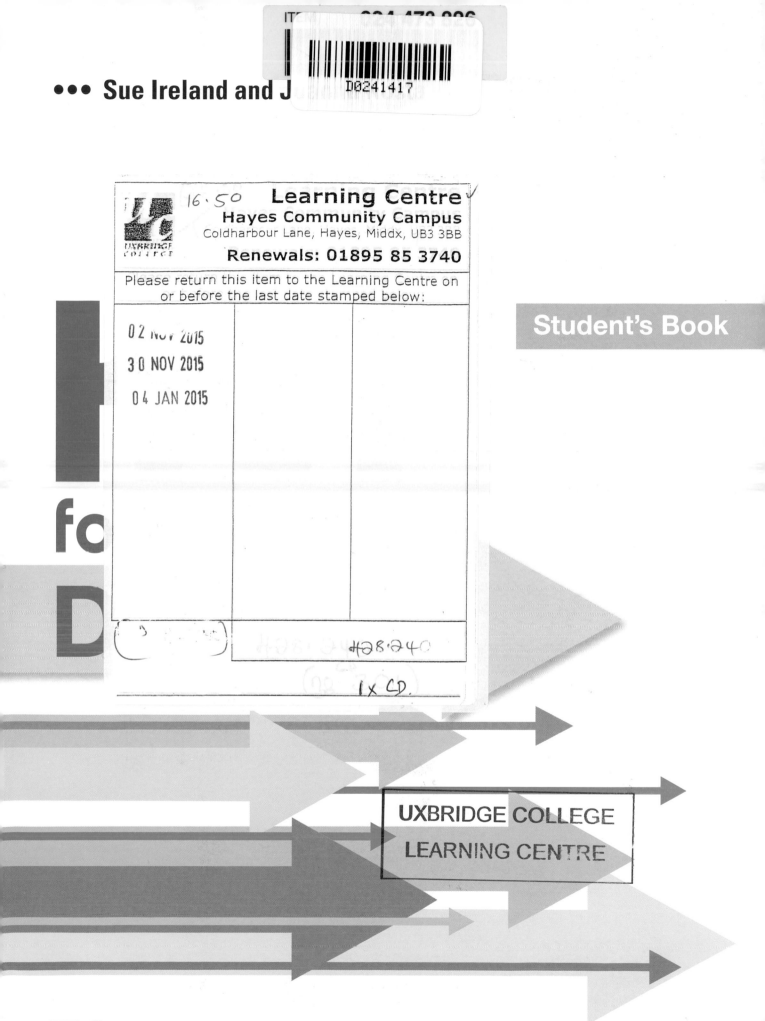

••• Sue Ireland and J

Student's Book

CAMBRIDGE
UNIVERSITY PRESS

Contents

Unit	Page	Unit title	Lesson	Exam practice
	p4	**Introduction**		
1	p6	**Different lives**	Where are you from?	• Listening Part 4 • Speaking Part 1
	p8		When do you have English?	• Listening Part 2 • Reading and Writing Part 2
2	p10	**Your family**	What does she look like?	• Listening Part 1
	p12		What does he do?	• Listening Part 2 • Speaking Part 1
3	p14	**Getting together**	Let's do something!	• Reading and Writing Part 3 (a) • Reading and Writing Part 7
	p16		Can you bring some drinks?	• Speaking Part 2 • Reading and Writing Part 8
	p18	**Review 1**		
4	p20	**My things**	I just got a T-shirt	• Listening Part 3 • Reading and Writing Part 2
	p22		The house where I live	• Reading and Writing Part 4
5	p24	**Food and drink**	We haven't got any milk	• Listening Part 5 • Reading and Writing Part 6
	p26		Are you ready to order?	• Reading and Writing Part 1
6	p28	**Entertainment**	They make him laugh	• Reading and Writing Part 3 (b) • Reading and Writing Part 4
	p30		Can you play the guitar?	• Listening Part 4 • Reading and Writing Part 9
	p32	**Review 2**		
7	p34	**Looking good**	I love these boots!	• Listening Part 5
	p36		He enjoys being in the parade	• Reading and Writing Part 4 • Reading and Writing Part 7
8	p38	**Look after yourself**	You might have the flu	• Reading and Writing Part 3 (b) • Reading and Writing Part 9
	p40		If you win the race…	• Reading and Writing Part 8 • Speaking Part 2
9	p42	**Planet Earth**	It's bigger than a cat	• Reading and Writing Part 5
	p44		It's going to rain	• Listening Part 1 • Reading and Writing Part 9
	p46	**Review 3**		
10	p48	**Going on holiday**	What are we doing on Saturday?	• Listening Part 5
	p50		The buses are too crowded	• Listening Part 3
11	p52	**Around town**	Have you been there?	• Listening Part 4 • Reading and Writing Part 4
	p54		Turn left at the traffic lights	• Reading and Writing Part 1 • Reading and Writing Part 7
12	p56	**The media**	I think technology is great	• Reading and Writing Part 5
	p58		An amazing story	• Speaking Part 2 • Reading and Writing Part 4
	p60	**Review 4**		
	p62	**Pairwork activities**	p68 **Exam guide** p96 **Language summary** p108 **Transcripts**	

Vocabulary	Language focus	Language booster
• countries, nationalities and languages • numbers and the alphabet	• introductions	• spelling
• school subjects, days and times	• present simple	• adverbs of frequency
• the family and describing people	• making questions	• *have got*
• talking about jobs	• present tenses	
• free time activities	• making suggestions	
• party things	• making offers and requests	• imperatives
• shopping	• past simple	
• the home	• relative pronouns	• *this, that, these, those*
• food	• countable and uncountable nouns	• plural nouns
• menus	• ordering food	
• films	• pronouns	• possessive '*s* and *s*'
• music	• modals for ability and obligation	
• clothes	• conjunctions	• *a pair of*
• festivals	• verbs with *-ing* or *to* + infinitive	
• health problems	• advice and possibility	• talking about how you feel
• sports	• first conditional	
• animals	• comparatives and superlatives	• irregular adjectives
• nature and the weather	• *going to* and *will*	
• holidays	• present continuous for future arrangements	
• transport	• *too* and *not enough*	• *too much* and *too many*
• buildings	• present perfect versus past simple	• *just, yet* and *already*
• places in town	• giving directions	
• technology	• *believe, hope, know, say* and *think*	
• books and reading	• past continuous	• *when* and *while*

p115 **Vocabulary list**

Introduction

About *KET* and *KET for Schools*

KET (Key English Test) is an exam set by University of Cambridge ESOL Examinations. It tests your ability to read, write, listen and speak in English. If you pass, you will get a qualification which shows that you have a basic knowledge of English and that you can do things like:

- ask questions to find out about someone's family or hobbies
- give facts about yourself
- talk about your likes and dislikes
- understand simple instructions
- follow simple travel directions.

KET for Schools is the same format as *KET*, but is for students aged between 11 and 14. It reflects the interests of young people, and includes topics like friends and family, shopping, sports and free time activities, animals, places, technology, and travel.

About *KET for Schools Direct*

KET for Schools Direct is a short, intensive course which will help you improve your English, practise the question types used in *KET for Schools*, and develop all the skills you need to pass the exam. There are 12 units in the book, each divided into two lessons. Each lesson looks at one of the topics which could appear in the exam.

Exam practice

Each lesson contains at least one exam task, so you will get plenty of opportunities to practise every part of the exam. The exam tasks are supported by *Exam tips* that give you useful advice on how to do that task, and at the back of the book there is an *Exam guide* (pages 68 to 95) which describes each part of the exam in detail. This includes an example of each part of the exam and gives more hints and tips on how to do it well. There are also lots of *Exam practice* questions in the *Workbook*. There is also a complete practice test in the *Workbook*.

Language focus and Vocabulary

In every lesson, you will learn some important vocabulary for the topic and you will practise key language points that could be used in the exam. There is also a *Language summary* section at the back of the book (pages 96 to 108), which looks at the language points covered in the lessons in more detail. You can get further practice of the language points and vocabulary in the *Workbook* and in the *Review* units.

The CD-ROM Exam Trainer

There are two ways you can use the CD-ROM. You can do a normal practice test under exam conditions, or you can use the *Exam Trainer* to get extra tips and advice for how to do each question. You can also print out your scores to see how you improve while you are studying.

Icons used in *KET for Schools Direct*

There is a list of the things you will practise in each lesson below the lesson title:

E = Exam skills
V = Vocabulary skills
L = Language skills

Each lesson also uses these icons:

🔊 07 This is the track number on the Teacher's CD.

✔70 This is a page reference to the *Exam guide*.

🔍 96 This is a page reference to the *Language summary*.

The format of the exam

Reading and Writing Paper

This paper takes 1 hour and 10 minutes. Parts **1-5** test your ability to read a variety of different texts and parts **6-9** test your writing ability.

Part	Task format	Number of questions	Exam guide
1	Match five sentences to eight notices.	5	p68
2	Choose the correct words to complete five sentences.	5	p70
3 (a)	Choose the correct answer to complete five short conversations.	5	p71
3 (b)	Fill five gaps in a conversation by choosing from eight possible answers.	5	p72
4	Read a text and choose the correct answers to seven questions.	7	p74
5	Choose the correct words to complete a text.	8	p76
6	Read the definitions and then write the words and spell them correctly.	5	p78
7	Write one word to fill each space in a short text.	10	p79
8	Read two texts and use the information to complete someone's notes.	5	p80
9	Write a short message which includes three pieces of information.	1	p82

Listening Paper

This paper takes about 30 minutes. You hear each part twice.

Part	Task format	Number of questions	Exam guide
1	Listen and choose the correct picture.	5	p84
2	Listen and match the questions to five of the eight possible answers.	5	p86
3	Listen and choose the correct answers to five questions.	5	p88
4	Listen to a conversation and complete some notes.	5	p90
5	Listen to one speaker and complete some notes.	5	p90

Speaking Paper

This paper lasts about 10 minutes. You do this part of the exam with one other candidate.

Part	Task format	Time	Exam guide
1	Answer the examiner's questions about you.	5-6 minutes	p92
2	Use the cards to ask and answer questions with your partner.	3-4 minutes	p94

1.1 Where are you from?

E Listening Part 4 · Speaking Part 1 | V countries, nationalities and languages · numbers and the alphabet | L introductions

Hi! My name's Sara and I'm 13 years old. I'm sailing around the world with my family. I love visiting different countries and meeting new people wherever I go. Here are some of my new friends.

Nice to meet you. I'm Paola. I'm from Rome. I'm thirteen.

Hi! I'm Dan. I'm from Sydney. I'm twelve years old.

Hello. I'm Carlos. I'm fourteen and I come from Mexico City.

Vocabulary: countries, nationalities and languages

1 Match the countries to the flags on the map.

> Argentina __   Australia __   Brazil __   Canada __   China __   Greece __
> Ireland __   Italy __   Mexico __   Poland __   Spain __   Thailand __

2 Write the nationality and language(s) for each country.

Brazil → Brazilian → Portuguese

3 Which countries are Sara's new friends from?
What nationalities are they? What languages do they speak?

(96) Language focus: introductions

4 Choose the best reply.

0 Hello.	A I'm thirteen.
1 How are you?	B Anthony, but call me Tony.
2 This is my friend Dan.	C I'm fine, thanks.
3 What's your name?	D Hi!
4 Where are you from?	E 41 Kellet Road.
5 How old are you?	F Nice to meet you.
6 What's your address?	G I'm from Scotland.

Vocabulary: numbers and the alphabet

02 **5** Listen and repeat the alphabet.

03 **6** Listen and write the letters that you hear. Then match the places to the descriptions.

0 S o __ __ __ __ __   __ __ __ __ __ __
1 __ __ __ __ __ __
2 __ __ __ __ __ __ __ __ __ __
3 __ __ __ __ __ __
4 __ __ __ __ __ __ __ __ __ __
5 __ __ __ __ __ __

A Australian city
B North American river
C Asian country
D South American country
E British city
F Italian city

04 **7** Listen and repeat the numbers.

11 12 13 14 15 16 17 18 19 20 21 32 43 54 65 76 87 98 100

05 **8** Listen and write the numbers.

0 _970_ years old   2 _____ people   4 _____ pages
1 Bus number _____   3 _____ minutes   5 _____ hours

Exam practice: Listening Part 4

06 **9** You will hear a teacher asking Sara for some information. Listen and complete each question.

STUDENT DETAILS

First name: _Sara_
Surname: **1** _____
Nationality: **2** _____
Age: **3** _____
Address: **4** 25 _____ Street
Phone number: **5** _____

Exam practice: Speaking Part 1

10 Put the words in the right order. When do you use these questions?

1 say / again / you / Can / that / ?
2 more / Can / that / say / you / slowly / ?
3 spell / you / How / that / do / ?

11 Ask two classmates questions to complete the forms.

1 STUDENT DETAILS

First name: _____
Surname: _____
Nationality: _____
Age: _____
Address: _____
Phone number: _____

2 STUDENT DETAILS

First name: _____
Surname: _____
Nationality: _____
Age: _____
Address: _____
Phone number: _____

When do you have English?

E Listening Part 2 • Reading and Writing Part 2 | V school subjects, days and times | L present simple

	Monday	Tuesday	Wednesday	Thursday	
9.10	Ⓐ	Ⓑ	Ⓒ	Ⓓ	
9.50	Ⓔ		Ⓕ		
10.30	BREAK				
10.45	Ⓖ	Ⓗ	Ⓘ	Ⓙ	
11.25				Ⓚ	

Vocabulary: school subjects, days and times

1 Match the school subjects to the pictures in the timetable.

Art __   Computer Studies __   Design __   Drama __   English __
French __   Geography __   History __   Maths __   Science __   Sport __

2 What classes do the students have...

1 at eleven twenty-five on Tuesday?
2 at a quarter to eleven on Thursday?
3 at ten to ten on Tuesday?
4 at ten past nine on Monday?
5 at nine fifty on Wednesday?
6 at half past ten every day?

Speaking

3 Work in pairs to complete Sue's timetable. Student A, look at page 62. Student B, look at page 65.

Exam tip ✓86

You will hear the things on the left in the same order as they are on the question paper.

Exam practice: Listening Part 2

07 **4** You will hear Maria asking Gary about their timetable for Friday. What time do they have each class? Write a letter (A–H) next to each time.

TIMES		SUBJECTS	
0	9.10 a.m.	_E_	A Art
1	9.50 a.m.	_____	B English
2	10.45 a.m.	_____	C Geography
3	11.25 a.m.	_____	D History
4	1.15 p.m.	_____	E Maths
5	1.55 p.m.	_____	F Music
			G Science
			H Sport

🔍 **96 Language focus:** present simple

5 Read the examples and match the two halves of the rules.

*What do we **have** at 1 o'clock? We **have** Geography.*
*Our History teacher always **gives** us lots of homework.*
*I **don't know** where my timetable is.*

1 We use the present simple to talk about
2 We add s to regular verbs for
3 We use *do* or *does* to make

A *he, she* and *it.*
B what we do every day.
C negative sentences and questions.

6 Use the present simple to complete the sentences in this interview with a young actor.

INTERVIEWER:	Tell me about your school, Jodie.
JODIE:	(0) _____ *I go* _____ (I / go) to a theatre school in London.
INTERVIEWER:	What subjects (1) _____ (you / study)?
JODIE:	Well, (2) _____ (I / study) subjects like English, Maths and Science, but (3) _____ (I / do) Drama, dance and singing too.
INTERVIEWER:	Which subject (4) _____ (you / like) best?
JODIE:	(5) _____ (I / love) Drama. (6) _____ (we / always have) a lot of fun.
INTERVIEWER:	(7) _____ (you / like) singing?
JODIE:	No, (8) _____ (I / hate) it! (9) _____ (my teacher / always tell) me I need to practise more.

7 Use the interview to write five sentences about Jodie.

Jodie goes to a theatre school in London.

Exam practice: Reading and Writing Part 2

8 Read the sentences about a boy on a football course. Choose the best word (A, B or C) for each space.

0 Tom _____ to the David Beckham Football Academy in the school holidays.
   (A) goes   B stays   C visits
1 On the first day, everyone _____ a free football shirt.
   A gives   B pays   C gets
2 The students _____ some of their lessons in a classroom.
   A make   B have   C let
3 There is a _____ at 11.00 a.m. for drinks and snacks.
   A stop   B delay   C break
4 They usually _____ matches in the afternoon.
   A practise   B play   C keep
5 Tom always has a _____ time on the course.
   A high   B great   C large

Speaking

9 Interview your partner about his or her usual school day.

A: What time do you get up?
B: I usually get up at seven.

2.1 What does she look like?

E Listening Part 1 | **V** the family and describing people | **L** making questions

Vocabulary: the family and describing people

1 Complete the family words with *a, e, i, o* and *u*.

0 *a u* nt
1 br __ th __ r
2 c ___ ___ s __ n

3 f __ th __ r
4 gr __ ndf __ th __ r
5 gr __ ndm __ th __ r

6 m __ th __ r
7 s __ st __ r
8 __ ncl __

2 Look at the family tree and complete the sentences.

children	daughter	husband	parents	son	wife

0 Molly is Dave's ___*wife*___.
1 Dave is Molly's _____.
2 Carl is Dave's _____.

3 Lucy and Carl are Molly's _____.
4 Lucy is Dave's _____.
5 Dave and Molly are Lucy's _____.

08 **3** Sophie is asking Jane about her family. Listen and match the names to the people in the picture.

0 Jane __*F*__
1 Alice ____

2 Tom ____
3 Ben ____

4 Colin ____
5 Dad ____

6 Granddad ____
7 Grandma ____

4 Write the words in the table. Some words can go in more than one category.

beautiful black blonde blue brown dark fair fat green
grey long old pretty red short tall thin white young

He/She's got ... eyes.   He/She's got ... hair.   He/She is ... .

blue

5 Describe the people in the family tree.

Molly's pretty. She's got short blonde hair and blue eyes.

have got

You can say *have got* or *have*:
I have got a brother.
I don't have a sister.

We usually use the short form of *have/has* with *got*:
I've got a brother.
He's got brown eyes.

🔍 (97) **Language focus:** making questions

6 Complete the questions with *how many, what, when, where, which* and *who*.

0 *How many* brothers have you got?   I've got one brother.
1 _____'s his birthday?   It's next month.
2 _____'s the other boy?   That's my cousin, Ben.
3 _____ one is your dad?   He's next to me.
4 _____ is your mum?   She's taking the photo.
5 _____ does she look like?   She's got long brown hair and glasses.

7 Make questions with these words. Then ask and answer the questions in pairs.

0 are there / how many people / in your family / ?

How many people are there in your family?

1 your grandparents / where / do / live / ?
2 are / how old / you / ?
3 got / have / what pets / you / ?
4 is / when / your mother's birthday / ?
5 who / your favourite singer / is / ?

🔊 (09) **Exam practice:** Listening Part 1

8 For each question, choose the right answer (A, B or C).

1 Which boy is Sam's brother?

Ⓐ   Ⓑ   Ⓒ

2 Who stayed with Jenny this weekend?

Ⓐ   Ⓑ   Ⓒ

3 Which man is Sally's grandfather?

Ⓐ   Ⓑ   Ⓒ

4 Which family are the new neighbours?

Ⓐ   Ⓑ   Ⓒ

Speaking

9 Write down the first names of some members of your family. Then ask and answer questions about your partner's family.

A: Who's Leo?
B: He's my cousin.
A: What does he look like?

Hi! I'm Rob. I go to Wood Street School, but I don't go to school on Saturdays. So today I'm watching a football match with my friends.

This is my older brother, Johnny. He's a police officer. He wears a uniform when he's working. He's not wearing it today. He's enjoying the football too.

My mum's a teacher in a school. She teaches young children. At the moment she's making a cake. She loves cooking.

Vocabulary: talking about jobs

1 Use the words in the box to talk about the jobs in the cartoons.

> boring   difficult   dirty   exciting   interesting   scary   tiring

Would you like to be a doctor?   No, it's a very difficult job.

2 Correct these silly sentences.

0	A builder	checks	a newspaper.
1	A dentist	cuts	aeroplanes.
2	A farmer	flies	animals.
3	A gardener	grows	cars.
4	A hairdresser	keeps	flowers and vegetables.
5	A journalist	looks after	houses.
6	A mechanic	builds	your hair.
7	A nurse	paints	pictures
8	A painter	repairs	sick people.
9	A pilot	writes for	your teeth.

0   *A builder doesn't check a newspaper. A builder builds houses.*

Reading

3 Read the cartoons about Rob and his family. What are their jobs? What are they doing now?

My dad's a doctor. It's his day off today, so he's not at the hospital. He's playing his guitar in a band with some friends.

 Language focus: present tenses

4 Read the examples and choose the correct words to complete the rules.

Present simple: *Rob's mother **teaches** children to read and write.*
Present continuous: *She **isn't teaching** now. She**'s making** a cake.*

1 We use the **present simple / present continuous** to talk about things we are doing now.
2 We use the **present simple / present continuous** to talk about things we often do.

5 Complete the mini-dialogues.

1 A: What does your dad do?
   B: (he / drive) _____ a taxi.
   A: Is he driving his taxi at the moment?
   B: No, (he / not be) _____.
      (he / eat) _____ his lunch.

2 A: What does your sister do?
   B: My sister (be) _____ a nurse, but
      she (not work) _____ today.
      She (paint) _____ a picture.

3 A: It's Sunday, so (we / not study) _____
      in school today.
   B: What (you / do) _____?
   A: (we / ride) _____ our bikes.

6 Ask your partner about his or her family.

What does your father / mother / aunt / uncle do?
What is he / she doing right now?

Exam tip ✓86

You might not hear the exact words you see in A-H. So, instead of 'cook', you might hear 'she gets the food ready in the kitchen.'

Exam practice: Listening Part 2

10 **7** Listen to Karen talking to her friend about the people in her family. What job does each person do? Write a letter (A − H) next to each person.

PEOPLE		JOBS	
0 dad	*A*	A	actor
1 mum	____	B	cook
2 sister	____	C	doctor
3 uncle	____	D	nurse
4 aunt	____	E	painter
5 cousin	____	F	receptionist
		G	teacher
		H	tour guide

Exam practice: Speaking Part 1

Exam tip ✓93

Try to keep talking until the examiner stops you.

8 The examiner may ask you about your family. Tell your partner about your family. Try to say at least five sentences.

My dad is a painter and my mum works for a bank.
I've got two brothers. Their names are...

3.1 Let's do something!

E Reading and Writing Part 3 (a) and Part 7 | **V** free time activities | **L** making suggestions

Vocabulary: free time activities

1 Complete the word wheels with the words.

baseball   the beach   the cinema   computer games   a DVD   a film
a restaurant   running   shopping   surfing   tennis   television

swimming   *a café*

play   **go**   **go to**   **watch**

football   *a football matc*

2 What do you usually do at the weekend? Tell your partner.

I sometimes play football with my friends.

Listening

3 Jo is talking to Sam about Saturday. Listen and circle their plans.

a.m.: *go shopping / go swimming*   **p.m.:** *play tennis / go to a restaurant*

4 Listen again and complete the dialogue with these phrases.

How about   Let's   Shall we   What about

Jo: Are you free this Saturday, Sam?.
SAM: Yes, I am.
Jo: Great! **(1)** _____ do something! **(2)** _____ going shopping?
SAM: That's a great idea. Where shall we meet?
Jo: **(3)** _____ meeting outside the station at half past ten?
SAM: OK. **(4)** _____ play tennis in the afternoon?
Jo: No, that sounds boring. **(5)** _____ going to a restaurant?
SAM: Yeah, OK. **(6)** _____ try that new pizza restaurant near the station.
Jo: Good idea!

Are you free this Saturday, Sam?

98 Language focus: making suggestions

5 Choose the correct words to complete the rules.

Let's do something! How about going to a restaurant?

1 We use *Let's…* and *Shall we…* with *-ing* / the infinitive without *to*.
2 We use *How about…* and *What about…* with *-ing* / the infinitive without *to*.

6 Complete the mini-dialogues with the correct forms of the words in the box.

do	go	go to	play	play	watch

1 A: Let's _____ something this weekend.
  B: OK. What about _____ surfing?
2 A: How about _____ the cinema tonight?
  B: That sounds great. Which film shall we _____?
3 A: Shall we _____ baseball on Saturday?
  B: No, I don't like baseball. What about _____ tennis?

Exam Practice: Reading and Writing Part 3 (a)

7 Complete the five conversations. Choose A, B or C.

1 Let's go surfing on Saturday.
  A Is he free?   B No, I don't.   C What time?
2 I love playing computer games.
  A Me too!   B Of course not.   C That's all right.
3 Can I speak to Chris?
  A Yes, I can.   B Just a moment.   C Is it you?
4 It's very hot in here.
  A Let's go somewhere else.   B Sorry I can't.   C Here you are.
5 Shall we watch a baseball match tomorrow?
  A Yes, we do.   B Sometimes.   C That's a great idea.

Exam practice: Reading and Writing Part 7

8 Complete this email. Write ONE word for each space.

To:	Chris
≡▼ Subject:	Party

Hi Chris,
How (0) __*are*__ you? It's great that you are coming to stay with me
(1) _____ the weekend. What about (2) _____ to the cinema on
Saturday? I looked on the website and there's a funny film on about
(3) _____ boy who becomes a farmer. (4) _____ I book tickets?
(5) _____ the evening we are invited (6) _____ a party. And don't
(7) _____ your swimming things because the pool is open on Sunday. I
know we'll (8) _____ lots of fun.
Oh yes, (9) _____ you give me your mobile number again?
See (10) _____ soon,
Miki

Speaking

9 In pairs, role-play a conversation between two friends making plans for the weekend.

Exam tip ✔71
First look at the question and think of some possible answers. Then read the three choices carefully and choose your answer.

Exam tip ✔79
Look at the words before and after each space to help you to decide on the answers.

Let's go to the park.

That sounds boring. What about going swimming?

Exam practice: Speaking Part 2

1 Make questions using the prompts. Then ask and answer the questions with your partner.

1 how old / you?
2 when / birthday?
3 you / like birthday parties?
4 what / kind of parties / like?

2 Work in pairs. Student A, look at page 62. Student B, look at page 65.

Vocabulary: party things

3 Match the words to the things in the picture.

balloon __	barbecue __	burger __	cake __	candles __	card __
CD __	chicken __	crisps __	cups __	disco __	drinks __
fruit juice __	glass __	ice cream __	pizza __	plate __	present __

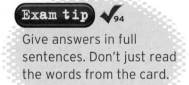

Shall I bring something to the party?

Can you bring some drinks?

Listening

4 You will hear Nicole talking to Tom about her party. What will each person bring?

| 0 Nicole | *crisps* | 2 Carl | _____ | 4 Tom | _____ |
| 1 Lisa | _____ | 3 Rosie | _____ | 5 Mike | _____ |

98 Language focus: making offers and requests

5 Read the sentences. Write *R* for *requests* (asking for help), and *O* for *offers* (giving help).

1 Can you bring some drinks? _____
2 Can I bring some plates? _____
3 Could you ask him to bring some music? _____
4 Shall I bring something to the party? _____

6 Complete the mini-dialogues with *shall I, can I, can you,* or *could you.*

1 A: _____ pour me a glass of orange juice?
   B: Sure. Pass me your glass.
2 A: _____ bring some drinks tonight?
   B: No, it's OK. We've already got some. _____ bring some crisps?
3 A: Let's make a birthday cake for Nicole.
   B: Good idea! Mum, _____ help us?
4 A: _____ make some sandwiches for the party?
   B: That'd be great. Don't forget to make some without meat.

Exam practice: Reading and Writing Part 8

7 Look at Steve's notes and find the answer that might be...

1 a time _____   3 a phone number _____
2 a place _____   4 a thing _____

8 Read the invitation and the email. Fill in the information in Steve's notes.

Come to my birthday party!

We're playing football at the Sports Centre on Saturday 5th April from 11 a.m. to 1.30 p.m. Please bring trainers (not boots). Can you come? Call me on 07864-011328 before Wednesday.

George

To: Steve
Subject: George's Party

Hi Steve,

I'm going to George's party, but I don't know where the sports centre is. Can you meet me at the station so we can walk there together? How about meeting at 10.45? Let me know. My new mobile is 07876-538724.

Harry

Steve's notes
George's Party
Date: (0) 5th April
Place: (1) _____
Meet Harry at: (2) _____ am
Meeting place: (3) _____
Harry's number: (4) _____
Must take: (5) _____

Speaking

9 Work in groups. Plan a party.

A: Let's have a Halloween party!
B: Yeah, that's a great idea. Shall I make some invitations?
A: OK. When shall we have the party?

Review 1

1 Circle the odd one out.

0	name	address	(eyes)	age
1	English	maths	timetable	science
2	thin	hair	short	pretty
3	Brazil	Canadian	French	Polish
4	sometimes	never	what	always
5	grey	brown	blond	old
6	doctor	cleaner	nurse	hospital
7	cake	burger	crisps	barbecue
8	husband	aunt	grandfather	son

2 Look at the people in the pictures. What are their jobs?

I work in a school.

0 ___teacher___

I write for a newspaper.

1 _____

Shall I cut your hair?

2 _____

Can I check your teeth?

3 _____

I fly aeroplanes.

4 _____

Can I fix your car?

5 _____

I am sometimes on TV.

6 _____

I paint pictures.

7 _____

3 Complete this conversation with the sentences below.

SAM: Hello, Marina. How are you?
MARINA: Hi, Sam. I'm fine thanks.
SAM: Marina, this is my pen-friend. She's staying with me for a week.
MARINA: (1) _____
BIRGIT: I'm from Germany. Pleased to meet you too, Sam. My name's Birgit.
MARINA: (2) _____
BIRGIT: It's Birgit. That's B-I-R-G-I-T. It's quite difficult for English people to say.
MARINA: (3) _____
BIRGIT: Really? Why? What's your surname?
MARINA: (4) _____
BIRGIT: Oh! So we have the same problem!
MARINA: (5) _____

A It's Pavlopoulos. My Dad comes from Greece.
B Sorry, can you say that again? How do you spell it?
C Well, don't worry, so is my surname.
D That's right!
E Oh hi, nice to meet you. Where are you from?

4 Put the words in the right order.

0 old / how / are / you / ?

___How old are you?___

1 your / birthday party / is / what time / ?

_____

2 balloons / are / the / where / ?

_____

3 pizzas / there / are / how many / ?

_____

4 shall / I / the / glasses / where / put / ?

_____

5 which CD / listen to / first / shall / we / ?

_____

6 who / is / your / birthday cake / making / ?

_____

5 Complete the sentences with the correct forms of the verbs.

be   come   go to   have   have got   ~~wear~~   work

0 My sister always _wears_ pink shoes.
1 My dad _____ blue eyes.
2 My grandparents _____ from China.
3 I _____ three cousins in Australia.
4 My brother _____ for a computer company.
5 My brother's girlfriend _____ very pretty.
6 My mum and I often _____ the cinema on Saturdays.

6 Look at the picture. What are the people doing?

Mr Smith is crying.

Mr Smith   Alan   Stefan   Chris   Hiro

Franco   Gloria   Tomas   Ian   Jane

7 Complete the dialogue with *in*, *on* and *at*.

STEVE: Hi, Dan. Are you going to Cath's party?
DAN: Yes, I am. Are you?
STEVE: Yes, but I don't know where my invitation is! Is the party this weekend?
DAN: No, it's **(1)** _____ Saturday 24th June. Her birthday's **(2)** _____ July but she's on holiday then.
STEVE: Oh, right. And it's **(3)** _____ the afternoon isn't it? **(4)** _____ 2 o'clock?
DAN: Actually, it's **(5)** _____ 2.30. Can you remember where it is?
STEVE: It's at Top Pin Bowling, isn't it?
DAN: That's right! The address is 24 High Lane.

8 Complete the rest of the dialogue with these phrases.

Can you   Let's   Shall we   What about

STEVE: **(0)** _____ _Shall we_ _____ buy the present together?
DAN: OK. What **(1)** _____ get her?
STEVE: I'm not sure. **(2)** _____ ask her sister what she wants.
DAN: Good idea. **(3)** _____ going shopping on Saturday?
STEVE: I need to ask my mum first. **(4)** _____ call me at home this evening?
DAN: No problem. Speak to you later, Steve.
STEVE: Bye, Dan.

On target?

How well can you do these things?	☆	☆☆	☆☆☆
E listen for times, dates, places and names			
E find key information in short emails, adverts and invitations			
E choose the right responses to questions or statements			
V talk about my life, my family and my school			
L spell words correctly and ask people to spell words			
L ask someone to repeat what they said			
L ask and answer questions			
L use the present simple and present continuous tenses			
L make and respond to offers, requests and suggestions			

E **Exam skills**   V **Vocabulary skills**   L **Language skills**

4.1 I just got a T-shirt

E Listening Part 3 · Reading and Writing Part 2 | **V** shopping | **L** past simple

Vocabulary: shopping

1 Match the words to the things in the picture.

cinema tickets ___ a comic book ___ a computer game ___ a DVD ___
a football shirt ___ a magazine ___ make-up ___ sweets ___ a pair of trainers ___

2 Where can you buy the things in the picture? What other things can you buy in these places?

bookshop   cinema   clothes shop   music shop
newsagent's   toyshop   sports shop   supermarket

Exam tip ✔88
Use the time before you listen to read all the questions carefully.

Exam practice: Listening Part 3

3 Liz is telling her father about the things she bought. Which things does she talk about.

4 Listen again and choose the right answer (A, B or C).

0 When did Liz go to the shopping centre?
  (A) today   B yesterday   C on Tuesday

1 What did Liz buy for the baby?
  A a ball   B a book   C a toy animal

2 What sort of CD did Liz choose?
  A pop music   B dance music
  C rock music

3 What clothes did Liz get?
  A some jeans   B a sweater   C a T-shirt

4 At lunchtime, Liz and Sally
  A had a picnic.   B ate in a snack bar.
  C went to a coffee shop.

5 Liz bought Dad's magazine
  A in the department store.
  B at a newsagent's.   C in a bookshop.

(99) **Language focus:** past simple

5 We use the past simple to talk about things that happened in the past and are now finished. Read the examples and complete the rules.

*The shopping centre **was** closed yesterday. All the shops **were** closed.*
***Did** you go to the coffee shop? No, we **didn't**. We **went** to the park.*
*I **looked** at some books. I **listened** to some CDs.*

1 The past forms of *be* are _____ and _____.
2 We use _____ to make questions in the past simple.
3 We use _____ to make negative sentences in the past simple.
4 We can make the past forms of some verbs by adding _____.

6 Complete the speech bubbles with the past simple forms of the verbs.

I hate shopping! I **(0)** ___went___ **(go)** into town last weekend because I
(1) _____ **(want)** to buy some new jeans last weekend, but the shops
(2) _____ **(be)** really busy and I **(3)** _____ **(not see)** anything I liked.
I **(4)** _____ **(try)** on a couple of pairs, but they **(5)** _____ **(not fit)** me.
Now I have to go again next weekend!

My friends and I go shopping every weekend. Last weekend we
(6) _____ **(meet)** at 10 o'clock and we **(7)** _____ **(spend)** all morning
looking at new clothes in the department store. Then we **(8)** _____ **(eat)**
lunch in our favourite coffee shop. In the afternoon, we **(9)** _____ **(decide)**
to look at CDs and then we **(10)** _____ **(have)** an ice cream. It was great!

Exam tip ✔70

Try all three options in the space before you choose your answer.

Exam practice: Reading and Writing Part 2

7 Read the sentences about going shopping. Choose the best word (A, B or C) for each space.

0 Carlos wanted to __*get*__ a new mobile phone.
  Ⓐ get   B spend   C make
1 He went to the department store because it had _____ prices.
  A little   B low   C small
2 He took the lift to the top _____ where they sold phones.
  A floor   B place   C stairs
3 The assistant showed him several phones but they were too _____ .
  A high   B rich   C expensive
4 Carlos _____ to buy a computer game instead.
  A thought   B decided   C knew
5 Carlos paid for the game and the assistant gave him some _____ .
  A bill   B card   C change

Speaking

8 Think of something you bought recently. In pairs, ask and answer questions about it. Can you find out what your partner bought?

When...?   Where...?   How much...?   What colour...?   Why...?

When did you buy it?

I bought it last month.

E Reading and Writing Part 4 | **V** the home | **L** relative pronouns

ROOM A

ROOM B

ROOM C

Vocabulary: the home

1 Do you live in a house or an apartment? Use the words in the box to talk about your home.

> apartment   bathroom   bedroom   dining room   garden
> garage   hall   house   kitchen   living room

2 Match the words to the things in the pictures.

> bath __   bed __   bookcase __   carpet __   ceiling __   chair __   computer __
> curtain __   desk __   door __   floor __   lamp __   light __   pillow __   poster __
> shelf __   shower __   sink __   sofa __   towel __   TV __   wall __   window __

3 Tell your partner about some of the rooms in your house.

In the living room we've got a large sofa, a TV, and...

Listening

4 Listen to Gina, Harry and Daniel talking about the rooms in the pictures. Match the people to the rooms.

1 Gina _____   2 Harry _____   3 Daniel _____

*There are several big chairs in here, **which** are really comfortable.*

*There's a desk with my computer on it, **where** I do my homework.*

*I've got a friend called James **who** plays the guitar.*

Language focus: relative pronouns

5 Read the examples and complete the rules.

1 We use _____ to give more information about a place.
2 We use _____ to give more information about a person.
3 We use _____ to give more information about a thing.

6 Complete the sentences with *where*, *which* or *who*.

1 My brother, _____ is ten, wants to paint his bedroom black.
2 I want to put my desk under the window, _____ there's more light.
3 Trisha, _____ loves music, has lots of posters of pop stars in her bedroom.
4 I've got a picture of a horse, _____ my grandmother painted.
5 I put your card on my shelf, _____ I keep all my special things.
6 My parents' room, _____ is on the second floor, is really big.

Exam tip ✓74

Always find the right part of the text for the question and read it carefully before choosing your answer.

Exam practice: Reading and Writing Part 4

7 Read the article about Jay Shafer. Are sentences 1–7 'Right' (A) or 'Wrong' (B)? If there is not enough information to answer 'Right' (A) or 'Wrong' (B), choose 'Doesn't say' (C).

Living small

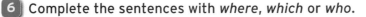

Jay Shafer's home is small but it has everything he needs to live comfortably. On the ground floor, there's a kitchen, a tiny bathroom with a toilet, and a room which he uses as a living room, work area and dining room. Upstairs there's a double bedroom. The kitchen has a sink, a fridge, a cooker and some cupboards. In the work area, there's a laptop and shelves full of books.

Everyone asks Jay why he wants to live like this. 'When I was a teacher, I lived in a big apartment. It had lots of rooms that I never used but I still had to clean them and pay for them,' he explains. 'So I decided to build myself a small house. It took me about two months, with some help from my friends.'

People were very interested in his new way of life. His story was told on TV and in newspapers and magazines all over the US. Now Jay has a new job, building little houses for other people. Not everyone lives in them of course – they put them in the garden or use them as holiday homes. 'It's my idea of a dream home' says Jay, 'but it's not right for everyone.'

Language booster

this, that, these, those

We use *this* and *these* for things that are near us:
This is my room.
These are my drums.

We use *that* and *those* for things that are not near us:
That's my sofa.
Those are my curtains.

0 Jay Shafer's house has everything except a bathroom.	A Ⓑ C
1 Jay's house has two floors.	A B C
2 Jay's bedroom is big enough for two people.	A B C
3 When Jay is in his house, he spends most of his time reading.	A B C
4 Jay needed all the rooms in his old flat.	A B C
5 Jay built his house by himself.	A B C
6 Jay enjoyed talking to journalists about his house.	A B C
7 People pay Jay to build houses for them.	A B C

Speaking

8 Draw a picture of your dream house and describe it to your partner.

This is my dream house. There is a big living room...

5.1 We haven't got any milk

E Listening Part 5 · Reading and Writing Part 6 | V food | L countable and uncountable nouns

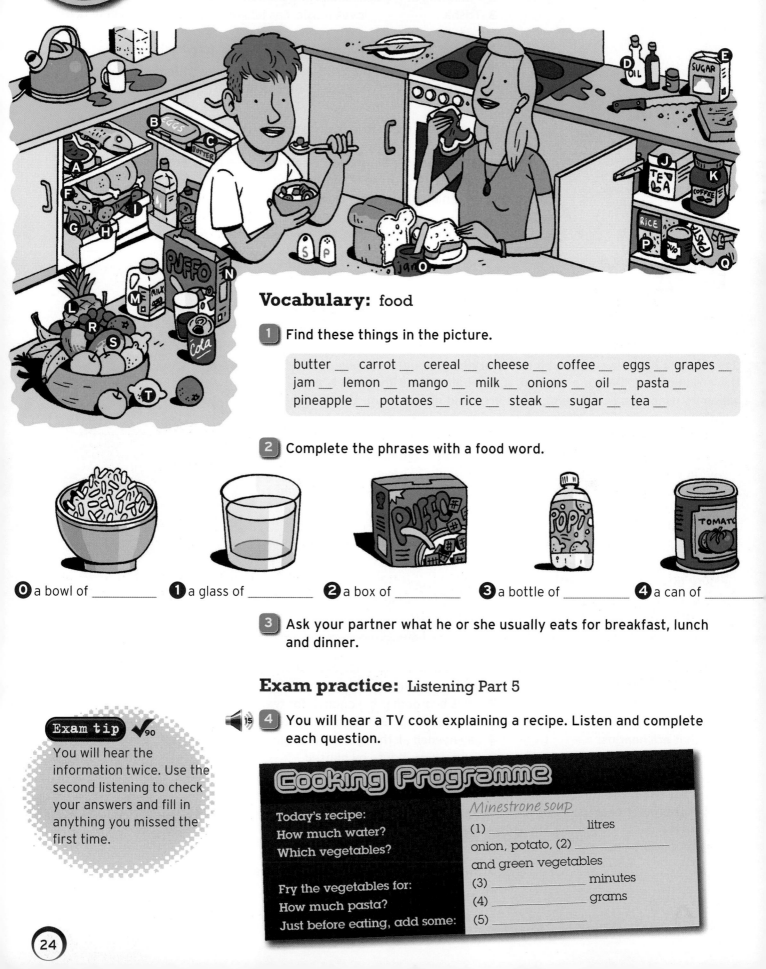

Vocabulary: food

1 Find these things in the picture.

> butter ___ carrot ___ cereal ___ cheese ___ coffee ___ eggs ___ grapes ___
> jam ___ lemon ___ mango ___ milk ___ onions ___ oil ___ pasta ___
> pineapple ___ potatoes ___ rice ___ steak ___ sugar ___ tea ___

2 Complete the phrases with a food word.

0 a bowl of _____ **1** a glass of _____ **2** a box of _____ **3** a bottle of _____ **4** a can of _____

3 Ask your partner what he or she usually eats for breakfast, lunch and dinner.

Exam practice: Listening Part 5

15 **4** You will hear a TV cook explaining a recipe. Listen and complete each question.

Exam tip ✔90

You will hear the information twice. Use the second listening to check your answers and fill in anything you missed the first time.

Cooking Programme

Today's recipe: **Minestrone soup**

How much water? (1) _____ litres

Which vegetables? onion, potato, (2) _____ and green vegetables

Fry the vegetables for: (3) _____ minutes

How much pasta? (4) _____ grams

Just before eating, add some: (5) _____

Can I have some tea?

Yes, you can have some tea.
How much tea do you want?

Are there any eggs?

No, there aren't any eggs.
How many eggs do we need?

Exam tip ✔78

Read the description carefully to see whether you need to write a singular or plural word.

You need: 4 slices of bread, a banana, butter, chocolate spread, peanut butter

Recipe: First take the skin off the banana and cut it into slices.

Then put some butter on the bread and make a sandwich with the banana slices.

Next put chocolate spread on top of the sandwich and put another slice of bread on top.

After that put peanut butter on top of that, and then put on the last slice of bread.

Finally, cut it in half and eat it!

🔍100 Language focus: countable and uncountable nouns

5 Read the rules and write C next to the countable nouns and U next to the uncountable nouns in Activity 1.

Countable nouns are things you can count.

Uncountable nouns are things you can't count.

6 Read the cartoons and choose the correct words to complete the rules.

1 We use *How many...?* to ask about **countable / uncountable** nouns.
2 We use *How much...?* to ask about **countable / uncountable** nouns.
3 We use **some / any** in factual questions and negative sentences.
4 We use **some / any** in questions that are requests or offers.
5 We use **some / any** in affirmative sentences with plurals and uncountable nouns.

7 Complete the dialogue with *some, any, how much* and *how many*.

SAM: Mum, can we have omelette for dinner tonight?
MUM: Good idea, Sam, **(1)** _____ milk have we got in the fridge?
SAM: We haven't got **(2)** _____ milk.
MUM: Oh. Well, can you go to the shop and buy **(3)** _____?
SAM: Sure. Do we need **(4)** _____ cheese? Shall I buy **(5)** _____ of that too?
MUM: No, there's lots of cheese. But can you buy me **(6)** _____ eggs?
SAM: OK. **(7)** _____ do you want?
MUM: Just one box. Thanks, Sam.

Exam practice: Reading and Writing Part 6

8 Read the descriptions of some food words. What is the word for each one? The first letter is already there. There is one space for each other letter in the word.

0 Some people have this yellow fruit in their tea.   l *emon*
1 You often have this on top of pizza.   c _____
2 Some people like to eat these fried at breakfast time.   e _____
3 This makes cakes and biscuits nice and sweet.   s _____
4 These are red and can be cooked or put in salads.   t _____
5 When you are very thirsty, you should drink this.   w _____

Writing

9 Read this recipe. Would you like to try this sandwich?

10 Write your own Monster Sandwich recipe. Who has the best idea?

Annette's Monster Sandwich

A YOUNG'S
Sunday Special
£10
1 pm – 10 pm
Eat as much as you can

B Mouchak Indian Restaurant Takeaway food 15% cheaper than eat-in menu

C Wait here. The waiter will take you to your table.

D Please put your dirty dishes on this shelf.

E This table is for members of staff only.

F Special Offer Plate of pasta, salad and drink £7.

G Japanese Sushi Bar Open for lunch and dinner Monday – Friday

H Pay for your food at the bar when you order

Exam tip ✔68

Be careful: some sentences may use the same words as the notices, but the meaning of the whole sentence might be different.

Exam practice: Reading and Writing Part 1

1 Look at the notices (A–H). Where can you see these notices?

2 Which notice (A–H) says this (1–5)?

0	You must pay for your meal before you eat it.	*H*
1	Our food costs less if you eat it at home.	____
2	We are closed at the weekend.	____
3	Don't leave your plate on the table at the end of your meal.	____
4	A member of staff will show you where to sit.	____
5	You don't pay extra for a glass of lemonade.	____

Vocabulary: menus

3 Write the words in the in the spaces (A–D) in the menu.

Desserts   Drinks   Main courses   Side dishes

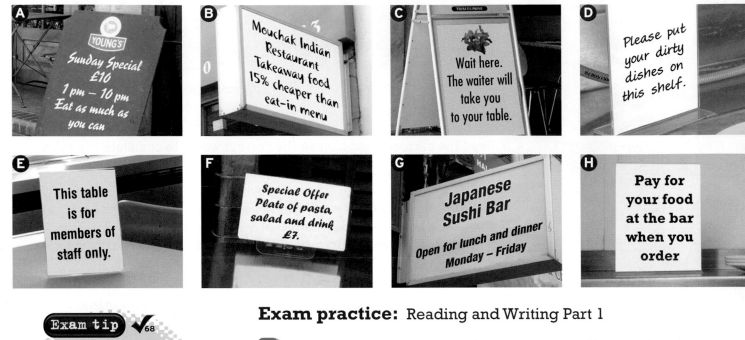

Happy Joe's Café

A _____
- Cheeseburger   £3.50
- Chickenburger   £3.50
- Veggieburger   £3.50
- Pizza   £5.75

Choose any four toppings: cheese, tomato, ham, mushrooms, onions, peppers, pineapple

C _____
- Ice cream   £2.50
  (strawberry, vanilla, chocolate)
- Chocolate brownie   £3.50
- Banana cake   £3.50
- Fresh fruit salad   £2.50

B _____
- Chips   £1.50
- Onion rings   75p
- Green salad   £1.75

D _____
- Fresh fruit juice   £1.00
  (orange, apple, grape, pineapple)
- Cola, Lemonade   £1.50

What's a chocolate brownie?

It's chocolate cake that's hard on top and soft inside. It's very good.

4 Make questions for the waiter's answers. Use *What is/are...?*, *What...have you got?*, *How much is/are...?*.

1 WAITER: It's made of vegetables. There's no meat in it.
2 WAITER: All kinds. You can choose any four toppings.
3 WAITER: It's £5.75.
4 WAITER: They're potato pieces cooked in hot oil.
5 WAITER: We've got strawberry, vanilla, and chocolate.

Listening

5 Mike and Amy are ordering some food at Happy Joe's Café. Listen and write down what they want to drink.

6 Listen again and circle all the things on the menu that they order.

Language focus: ordering food

7 Read the sentences. Write C for things the customer says and W for things the waiter says.

1 I'd like a cheeseburger please. _____
2 Would you like some chips? _____
3 I'll have a salad. _____
4 Do you want any side dishes? _____
5 Can I have a glass of water? _____
6 A chocolate brownie for me, please. _____
7 What about a dessert? _____
8 Are you ready to order? _____

8 Match the sentences with the same meanings.

1 I like chocolate.   A I want some chocolate.
2 I'd like some chocolate.   B I think chocolate's great.

9 Choose the correct words to complete the dialogues.

0 A: Do you like / Would you like fish?
  B: I do, but I don't eat it very often.
1 A: What **do you like / would you like** on your pizza?
  B: I'll have ham, pineapple and cheese.
2 A: **I like / I'd like** a chickenburger with chips please.
  B: OK. Do you want chips with that?
3 A: **Would you like / Do you like** Mexican food?
  B: I don't know. I've never tried it.
4 A: **Do you like / Would you like** a boiled egg for breakfast?
  B: Yes please, and some bread and butter.

Speaking

10 Role play a conversation in a restaurant. Use the menu from Happy Joe's Café. One person is the waiter. The other people are customers.

A: Are you ready to order?
B: Yes. I'd like a chickenburger please.

6.1 They make him laugh

E Reading and Writing Part 3 (b) • Part 4 | **V** films | **L** pronouns

A

B

C

D

E

F

G

H

Vocabulary: films

1 **Match the words to the film posters.**

an action film ___   an adventure film ___   a comedy ___   a fantasy ___
a horror film ___   a romance ___   a science fiction film ___   a thriller ___

2 **Match the phrases to the pictures below.**

It was boring. ___   It was exciting. ___   It was funny. ___
It was interesting. ___   It was sad. ___   It was scary. ___
It was strange. ___   It was terrible. ___   It was wonderful. ___
It made me cry. ___   It made me smile. ___   It made me laugh. ___

A   B   C   D   E

Exam practice: Reading and Writing Part 3 (b)

3 **Complete the conversation between two friends. What does Gary say to Dave?**

DAVE: Hi, Gary. Do you want to go to the cinema this weekend?
GARY: 0   *D*
DAVE: Just Tim and Elle.
GARY: 1 _____
DAVE: I'm not sure. What sort of thing do you like?
GARY: 2 _____
DAVE: I like science fiction, but I know Elle hates it.
GARY: 3 _____
DAVE: Good idea. What time is best for you?
GARY: 4 _____
DAVE: Fine, I'll tell Tim and Elle. Will you check the film times?
GARY: 5 _____
DAVE: Thanks. I'll speak to you later, Gary. Bye.

A Sure, I'll do that tonight.
B Great! I like them. What film shall we see?
C Saturday afternoon – I've got football practice on Sunday.
D Yeah, OK. Who are you going with?
E Anything except romance! What about you?
F What time does that film start?
G Well, what about that new thriller? I heard it's really exciting.
H Are they friends of yours?

Exam practice: Reading and Writing Part 4

4 Read the information about three young actors and then answer the questions. Choose A for Emma, B for Daniel and C for Rupert.

Emma Watson was born on April 15th 1990. From the age of three she knew she wanted to be an actor, but before she got the part of Hermione in the Harry Potter films, she only acted in school plays. When she is not acting, Emma loves to study and she is also good at hockey. Emma lives with her mother and her younger brother, Alex. Her favourite actors are Julia Roberts, John Cleese and Sandra Bullock.

Daniel Radcliffe was born in 1989 and has no brothers or sisters. He was in two films before he was chosen to play the part of Harry Potter. He is not very sporty and doesn't like studying, but he has a lot of CDs and always has his MP3 player with him. He says he does not know how much money he has earned playing Harry Potter and says that being rich and famous has not changed him at all.

Rupert Grint was born in 1988. He is the eldest of five children. Playing the part of Ron Weasley was his first acting job, but before that he was once in a school play. In his free time he plays the guitar and watches football on TV. His favourite actor is Jim Carey and he loves films that make him laugh, like *Shrek* and *Ace Ventura*. He also loves buying things with all the money he has earned!

0 Who decided to be an actor at a very early age?	Ⓐ B C
1 Who enjoys spending money?	A B C
2 Who listens to a lot of music?	A B C
3 Who plays a sport well?	A B C
4 Who enjoys doing school work?	A B C
5 Who likes watching comedies?	A B C
6 Who has several brothers and sisters?	A B C
7 Who worked as an actor before being in the Harry Potter films?	A B C

Language focus: pronouns

5 Read the instructions and colour the circles.

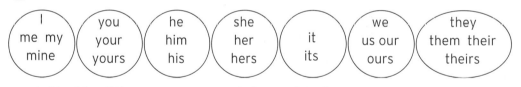

| I me my mine | you your yours | he him his | she her hers | it its | we us our ours | they them their theirs |

1 Use blue if the pronouns can only be used for boys.
2 Use pink if the pronouns can only be used for girls.
3 Use green if the pronouns can be used for boys or girls.
4 Use red if the pronouns cannot be used for boys or girls.

6 Complete the sentences with a pronoun.

1 _____ watched _____ favourite actor's new film.
2 _____ was a good film but I can't remember _____ name!
3 _____ chairs were very uncomfortable, but _____ were fine.
4 _____ dropped _____ popcorn on the floor, but _____ didn't drop _____.
5 _____ ate all _____ sweets!

Speaking

7 Write some sentences about an actor then read them to your partner. Can your partner guess who it is?

She's about 30 years old. She has long dark hair...

Can you play the guitar?

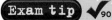

Music Survey

- What kind of music do you like?
- What are your favourite bands?
- Who is your favourite singer?
- How do you listen to music: on an MP3 player, on a CD player, or online?
- Can you play an instrument?
- Does anyone in your family play an instrument?
- Would you like to play an instrument?
- Which instrument would you like to learn?

Vocabulary: music

1 **Match the types of music to the photos.**

1 rock _____	3 dance _____	5 hip hop _____
2 pop _____	4 reggae _____	6 classical _____

2 **Find these instruments in the pictures.**

drums   electric guitar   keyboard   piano   violin

3 **Ask and answer the questions in the music survey.**

Exam practice: Listening Part 4

4 **You will hear a boy asking about music lessons. Listen and circle the numbers you hear.**

- 9.00   9.30   10.00   10.30
- 6   16   12   20
- £13.50   £17.50   £30.00   £35.00   £157.00   £175.00
- 2nd   3rd   7th   13th

5 **Listen again and complete each question.**

Exam tip ✔90

Listen carefully. You may hear two times, prices or dates, but only one will be correct.

Music Lessons

Name of school:	Dave Martin's School of Rock
Guitar lessons on:	(1)
Time of class:	(2) _____ am
Largest class size:	(3) _____ people
Price per lesson:	(4) £ _____
Course start date:	(5) _____ March

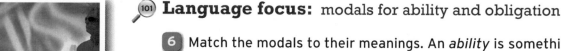

Language focus: modals for ability and obligation

6 Match the modals to their meanings. An *ability* is something we can do. An *obligation* is something we have to do.

0 *Can you play the guitar?*
1 *You* **need to** *come to the class at 9.30.*
2 *You* **don't have to** *bring anything to the lesson.*
3 *We* **must** *have six people in the class.*
4 *You* **needn't** *pay today.*
5 *I* **could** *play the piano when I was four.*
6 *I* **had to** *buy a music book for the course.*

A past ability
B present obligation
C past obligation
D no obligation
E present ability

7 Choose the correct words to complete the rules.

1 To talk about **must** in the past, we use **had to** / **needn't**.
2 To talk about **can** in the past, we use **could** / **had to**.

8 Choose the correct words to complete the sentences.

1 I **mustn't** / **can't** play an instrument, but I'm a good singer.
2 You **couldn't** / **needn't** buy your own guitar. You can use the school's.
3 I **could** / **must** play the piano when I was younger.
4 I **have to** / **need** book my place on the course by tomorrow.
5 These days, you **can** / **must** download music from the internet.
6 You **mustn't** / **don't have to** buy CDs if you don't want to.
7 When my father was young, he **needn't** / **couldn't** download music.
8 He **must** / **had to** buy records or CDs in a music shop.

Exam practice: Reading and Writing Part 9

9 In groups, read the poster and talk about the things you need to do before you go this festival and the things you can do there.

We have to ask our parents first. We can buy some cool t-shirts.

Over 150 fantastic bands, including The Killers, CSS and Slipknot.

Choose your campsite: "Pur... ...people who want to stay up late or "Quieter Campsite" for people who need to sleep!

Lots of great shops: You can buy food, drinks, clothes and CDs.

READING Festival

22ⁿᵈ – 24ᵗʰ August

Prices: One-day ticket = £65.00, Weekend ticket = £155

Travel: Get the train to Reading station then take a bus, or you can drive.

For more information, see *www.readingfestival.com*

Exam tip ✔82

Remember to start your note with *Dear...* or *Hi...* and finish it with *Best wishes,* or *From,* and your name.

10 You want to invite your friend Sam to go to a music festival with you. Write an email to your friend. Say:
  – **when** the festival is on
  – **how** you can travel there
  – **what** you need to take
Write 25–35 words.

Review 2

1 Make words and then put them in the correct circle.

Starts of words		
~~but~~	chic	cof
com	coo	cup
fan	gui	key
mir	pep	pia
pic	piz	thri
vio		

End of words		
board	board	
edy	fee	ken
ker	ller	lin
no	per	ror
tar	tasy	~~ter~~
ture	za	

food and drink

butter

furniture

musical instruments

kinds of film

2 Read the clues and write the correct words.

0 It's a shop where you can buy books and magazines. _a bookshop_

1 This is a person who says "Are you ready to order?" _____

2 These are a kind of food which people often eat with burgers. _____

3 It's a room where people cook food.

_____

4 This is a shop which sells newspapers and magazines. _____

5 This is the kind of music which Queen, U2 and Muse play. _____

6 This is a place where you can buy lunch or dinner. _____

3 Complete the sentences about film ratings in the UK with *can* or *have to*.

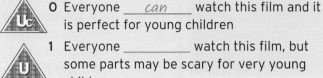

0 Everyone ___can___ watch this film and it is perfect for young children

1 Everyone _____ watch this film, but some parts may be scary for very young children.

2 Children _____ watch this film, but some parts may be scary for under eights.

3 If you are younger than twelve, you _____ watch this film with your parents.

4 You _____ watch this film if you are twelve years old or older.

5 You _____ be fifteen or over to watch this film.

6 Only people eighteen years old and over _____ see this film.

4 Complete the conversation between Fiona and her mum with these words.

any	any	How many	How much
~~How much~~	some	some	There's	They are

FIONA: Mum, I'd like to cook dinner tonight. I want to make baked chicken and potatoes.

MUM: That sounds very nice. (0) _How much_ chicken do you need?

FIONA: Four pieces, one for each person. I'll get them. Have we got (1) _____ potatoes?

MUM: Yes lots. (2) _____ do you want?

FIONA: Two large ones. And have we got (3) _____ lemons?

MUM: (4) _____ one in the fruit bowl.

FIONA: That's fine. Then I just need (5) _____ garlic.

MUM: (6) _____? I've only got two or three pieces

FIONA: That'll be enough. And I need (7) _____ pepper and salt and a little oil.

MUM: (8) _____ all in the cupboard.

FIONA: OK. Thanks, Mum.

5 Complete the article with the past simple form of the verbs.

Disney Animation Tour!

By Aaron Henderson, 11

Last month I **(0)** ___went___ **(go)** to Los Angeles in the US on a Disney trip. I **(1)** _____ **(have)** a special tour of the Disney cartoon library and studios.

I **(2)** _____ **(see)** some of the first drawings for Snow White. They **(3)** _____ **(draw)** them in 1937. They **(4)** _____ **(keep)** them in a special underground room which is always the same temperature as the paper is not very strong now.

The guide **(5)** _____ **(take)** us to see the first plans for Jungle Book. There **(6)** _____ **(be)** an extra character in them, a rhino called Rocky, but they **(7)** _____ **(cut)** him out of the film in the end. I **(8)** _____ **(learn)** some interesting facts about the Disney artwork and they **(9)** _____ **(show)** us how they made The Nightmare before Christmas. It **(10)** _____ **(be)** amazing!

6 Complete the mini-dialogues with the correct pronouns.

0 A: Is Mike eating a banana?
   B: No, _he_ is drinking a bottle of milk.

1 A: Is this Karen's CD?
   B: Yes, that's _____ CD.

2 A: Has Robin got a comic book?
   B: Yes, _____ has.

3 A: Is this Karen's magazine?
   B: Yes, it's _____.

4 A: What is Mike wearing?
   B: _____ is wearing _____ favourite foolball shirt.

5 A: Where are Robin, Mike and Karen?
   B: _____ are in _____ houses.

Mike   Karen   Robin

On target?

How well can you do these things?	☆	☆☆	☆☆☆
E understand the basic meaning of signs and notices			
E find and understand information in a reading text			
E listen and complete someone's notes			
V talk about my house and my bedroom			
V order food and go shopping			
V talk about films and music			
L use the simple past tense			
L talk about abilities and obligations			
L use pronouns correctly			

E Exam skills   V Vocabulary skills   L Language skills

7.1 I love these boots!

E Listening Part 5 | **V** clothes | **L** conjunctions

Vocabulary: clothes

1 Match the speech bubbles to the pictures.

1 __

> I love this pair of boots because I can wear them with a skirt or with trousers and a top. I chose them myself and bought them with my own pocket money. If it's cold I wear a jacket or I put on a warm coat. I don't like dresses so I never wear them.

2 __

> I wear these shorts when I go to the beach for surfing with my friends and I take a sweater because it's cold afterwards. I really like this cap and the sunglasses.

3 __

> I don't like wearing these trousers or this shirt and tie but they're part of my school uniform. I always put on jeans and a T-shirt when I get home. I'm glad we can wear trainers to school because I like them.

2 Underline the clothes words in the speech bubbles. Then write the words in the table. Can you add any more words?

On your head	On your hands	On your body	On your legs	On your feet
		shirt		

(102) **Language focus:** conjunctions

3 Look at the speech bubbles in Activity 1 and complete these sentences with *and, or, but, because, so, when,* and *if.*

1 *I don't like wearing these trousers or this shirt and tie _____ they're part of my school uniform.*
2 *_____ it's cold I wear a sweater _____ I put on a coat.*
3 *I love this pair of boots _____ I can wear them with a skirt or with trousers.*
4 *I don't like dresses _____ I never wear them.*
5 *I always wear these shorts _____ I go to the beach.*

4 Match the two halves of the sentences.

0 Lisa wasn't happy because   A he forgot to take the price off.
1 Leo looked great in a suit when   B swimming shorts at the beach.
2 Scott's socks had holes so   C she couldn't wear her best shoes.
3 Lisa had a little silver bag and   D his mum bought six new pairs.
4 Scott wore his new jeans but   E he went to his brother's wedding.
5 Leo usually wears shorts or   F her friend wore a silver belt.

Exam practice: Listening Part 5

5 Look at the notes about the Museum of Fashion. Which kinds of answers will you need? Where will they go?

A a price _____   C a place name _O_   E a spelling _____
B a time _____   D a clothes word _____   F a number _____

18 **6** You will hear some information about a fashion museum. Listen and complete each question.

Museum of Fashion

In: (0) Bath
Number of rooms: (1) _____
Special exhibition: 18th and 19th century (2) _____
Museum opens at: 10 a.m.
Closes at: (3) _____ at weekends
Family ticket costs: £ (4) _____
Car park in: (5) _____ Street

Speaking

7 Read the school uniform rules on the notice board. Would you like to go to this school?

8 In groups, make some school uniform rules for a different school.

Football School Rules
- Students must always wear football shirts, shorts, socks and football boots.
- Students must have their name and number on the back of their football shirts so teachers know who they are.
- Students must not wear trousers when it is cold.

He enjoys being in the parade

E Reading and Writing Part 4 and Part 7 | **V** festivals | **L** verbs with *-ing* or *to* + infinitive

by Simone Watkins (age 13)

London's Notting Hill Carnival is the biggest street festival in Europe. There are large festivals in Germany too, but only the carnival in Rio in Brazil is bigger.

It's on the last weekend in August and more than fifty bands and discos drive through the streets on trucks playing really loud West Indian music. My granddad is eighty now and he's played in every carnival since it began forty-five years ago. My dad's in a reggae group and he's teaching me to play the drums. I want to have my own band one day.

Between the bands there are parades of dancers in fantastic costumes. My family all dance with Dad's band. Mum starts planning the costumes a year before and my sister and I help her to make them during the school holidays. This year Mum and I have pink dresses and tights, with a white belt and cap. The boys have pink suits too. My brother says he hates the colour but he still enjoys being in the parade.

My older sister's costume is a swimsuit with lots of gold and silver decorations, and silver shoes. Her head-dress is very heavy and almost a metre high – she found dancing in it difficult at first. I love getting ready for the carnival. That's why I never feel sad when it ends because I know we'll soon start to make plans for the next one!

Vocabulary: festivals

1 Find these things in the photographs.

a band	costumes	crowds	dancers	drums
a festival	food	a headdress	a lorry	a parade

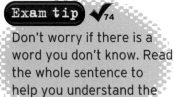

Don't worry if there is a word you don't know. Read the whole sentence to help you understand the meaning.

Exam practice: Reading and Writing Part 4

2 Read the article about the Notting Hill Carnival and answer the questions.

0 The biggest street festival in the world is in
  A London.
  B Germany.
  C Rio.

1 How many carnivals has Simone's grandfather been in?
  A 45.
  B 50.
  C 80.

2 Simone hopes to
  A join her father's band.
  B learn to play an instrument.
  C have her own band.

3 What does Simone say about her mother?
  A She no longer dances in the carnival.
  B She spends a year making the costumes.
  C She works as a school teacher.

4 Simone's carnival cap is the same colour as her
  A dress.
  B belt.
  C tights.

5 Simone's brother doesn't like
  A dancing with his sisters.
  B helping his mother.
  C wearing his costume.

6 Simone's sister had problems dancing because
  A her headdress was so large.
  B her shoes were so high.
  C her dress was so heavy.

7 How does Simone feel at the end of the carnival?
  A Tired after so much work.
  B Excited about the next one.
  C Glad that it's finished.

🔍⁽¹⁰²⁾ Language focus: verbs with *-ing* or *to* + infinitive

3 Write the verbs in the table.

> I'm **learning** to play the drums.
> He **enjoys** being in the parade.
> I **hope** to go again next year.

> My brother **hates** wearing pink.
> I **want** to have my own band one day.
> I **love** getting ready for the carnival.

verbs followed by *to* + infinitive	verbs followed by *-ing* form
learn	*hate*

4 Complete the dialogue with the right forms of the verbs.

A: (0) *I want to go* (I / want / go) to the carnival. Will you come with me?
B: Sure. (1) _____ (I / love / go) to festivals.
A: (2) _____ (your sister / want / come) too?
B: I don't think so. (3) _____ (she / hate / be) in crowds.
A: That's too bad. (4) _____ (I / enjoy / be) with lots of people and _____ (dance) in the street.
B: Me too. And (5) _____ (I / like / try) all the different snacks from the food-sellers, don't you?
A: Yeah. Let's go! (6) _____ (we / not want / miss) anything.

5 Ask your partner about special days in their town or city.

What special days do you have? Which is your favourite day?
What do you love / like / enjoy doing? What do you hate doing?

Exam practice: Reading and Writing Part 7

6 Complete this letter. Write ONE word for each space.

Dear Simone,
I enjoyed reading (0) ___*about*___ your carnival. In Japan, the second Monday of January is a special day, (1) _____ nineteen-year-olds become adults.
We start (2) _____ ready very early in the morning (3) _____ we have to wear a beautiful kimono. My mother helps me to put (4) _____ on. We also wear white socks and wooden shoes. It's much easier (5) _____ men. They just need (6) _____ dark suit.
We all go (7) _____ a ceremony at the Town Hall and afterwards (8) _____ is a party.
I enjoy wearing our national costume (9) _____ it's not very comfortable. (10) _____ you like it?
Love, Mari

Speaking

7 Choose three words and make up your own festival! Then tell a classmate about your festival.

| clown | costume | dance | drums | fireworks | parade | snacks |

*Everyone **dances** in the street. There are **clowns** selling funny hats.*

8.1 You might have the flu

E Reading and Writing Part 3 (b) and Part 9 | V health problems | L advice and possibility

What's wrong? ❶○

I feel really sick and my stomach hurts!

What's the matter? ❷○

DOCTOR OF MEDICINE

I've got a terrible pain in my ear.

I had an accident when I was cycling to school.

Are you OK?

❸○

What's the matter? ❹○

I don't feel very well. I've got a temperature and a headache.

Talking about how you feel

We use *have got* with nouns:
I've got a headache.
I've got a cold.

We use *feel* with adjectives:
I feel sick.
I don't feel well.

Vocabulary: health problems

1 Find the parts of the body in the pictures.

arm	back	ear	eye	face	foot	hand
head	leg	mouth	neck	nose	stomach	

🔊 19 **2** Match the advice to the cartoons. Then listen to check your answers.

A It looks very red. You should take this medicine three times a day.
B Why don't you go home and rest? You might have the flu.
C It might be something you ate. You should rest and drink some water.
D You should go to hospital for an X-ray. Your arm may be broken.

🔍103 **Language focus:** advice and possibility

3 Read the examples and complete the rules.

*Why don't you go home and rest? You **might** have the flu.*
*You **should** go to hospital for an X-ray. Your arm **may** be broken.*

1 We use _____ and _____ to give someone advice
2 We use _____ and _____ when we're not sure.
3 We use these phrases with the **infinitive (without *to*) / -*ing*** form.

4 Complete the article with *should/shouldn't*, *may/may not* and *might/might not*.

How to get a good night's sleep!

1 You _____ try to go to bed at the same time every night.
2 You _____ have a TV in your bedroom.
3 You _____ play computer games just before you go to bed.
4 You _____ sleep well if you watch TV late at night.
5 You _____ feel sleepy if you listen to quiet music at bedtime.
6 You _____ eat chocolate or drink soft drinks before going to bed.

Exam tip ✔72

Make sure the sentence you choose fits with what comes before **and** after the sentence.

Exam practice: Reading and Writing Part 3 (b)

5 Complete the phone conversation between two friends. What does Greg say to Mike?

MIKE: Hi, Greg. Sorry to hear you're in hospital! What happened?
GREG: 0 __F__
MIKE: Oh no! How long will you be in hospital?
GREG: 1 _____
MIKE: That's good. So will you be back at school on Monday?
GREG: 2 _____
MIKE: You're so lucky! You're going to miss so many boring lessons!
GREG: 3 _____
MIKE: What a pity! Well, I'll help you with it.
GREG: 4 _____
MIKE: I'll tell him. We might visit you next week.
GREG: 5 _____
MIKE: Good idea!

A Thanks, Mike. Does Pete know what happened?
B I know. I'm really happy about that.
C Cool. Why don't you ask my mum if that's OK?
D But I'm not! Mr Hartley says I should study at home.
E The doctor wants me to stay at home for two weeks.
F Oh hi, Mike. I fell off my bike and broke my leg.
G They might let me go home on Sunday.
H I may be here for another month.

Exam practice: Reading and Writing Part 9

Exam tip ✔82

Write in full sentences, using correct punctuation (e.g. capital letters, full stops and question marks).

6 Read this email from your friend Mike.

From:	Mike
To:	

Greg has broken his leg and he wants me to visit him at home. Would you like to come with me? When shall we go? What present should we get him?

Write an email to Mike and answer the questions. Write 25–35 words. Start like this 'Dear Mike, I'd love to...'

Speaking

7 Work in pairs. Student A, look at page 63. Student B, look at page 66. Talk about some health problems and give some advice.

A: What's the matter?
B: My foot hurts!
A: You may need an X-ray.

If you win the race...

E Reading and Writing Part 8 · Speaking Part 2 | **V** sports | **L** first conditional

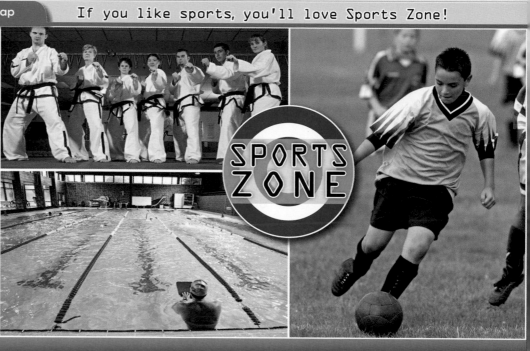

Our courses **Opening times** **Map**

If you like sports, you'll love Sports Zone!

Vocabulary: sports

1 Look at the courses menu in the website. Which of these sports can you do at Sports Zone?

baseball   basketball   climbing   fishing   football   gymnastics
hockey   horse-riding   karate   running   sailing   swimming
skiing   skateboarding   snowboarding   surfing   tennis   volleyball

2 Read the pages from the website. Which sports are these?

A
This course will teach you to use your mind as well as your body. It's not easy, but if you work hard you'll do well. There's a test at the end of the course and if you pass, you'll get a new belt, and move up to the next level.

B
Some people are afraid to try this because they think it's dangerous. But if you listen carefully and do everything correctly, you won't hurt yourself. We have very good teachers and the best wall in town, so come and try it!

C
This is a great team sport and the course is lots of fun. It doesn't matter what level you are, beginner or advanced; if you can run and jump, you're welcome to join us. And if you're tall, we'll be really happy to see you!

3 Ask and answer these questions in pairs.

1 Which sports do you like watching?
2 Which sports do you like doing?
3 How often do you do them?
4 Would you like to join Sports Zone?
5 Which sport would you like to learn? Why?

 **Language focus:** first conditional

4 Read the examples and choose the correct words to complete the rules.

> ┌─── if clause ───┐ ┌── main clause ──┐
> *If you work hard,* *you will do well.*
> ┌── main clause ──┐ ┌─── if clause ───┐
> *You won't hurt yourself* *if you are careful.*

1 We use the first conditional to talk about things that are **likely / unlikely** to happen in the future.
2 The verb in the **main clause / *if* clause** is in the present tense.
3 The verb in the **main clause / *if* clause** uses *will* + infinitive without *to*.

5 Make first conditional sentences.

1 if / play football in the rain / get very dirty
2 make new friends / if / join the football team
3 if / finish the course / get a certificate
4 get a silver cup / if / win the race
5 if / watch TV all day / not be very healthy
6 if / walk to school / get fit

6 What *will* or *won't* happen if you *do* or *don't do* these things?

1 eat a lot of fast food
2 learn a new sport
3 join a sports club
4 go to bed late every day
5 stop taking the bus
6 stay indoors all the time

Exam practice: Reading and Writing Part 8

7 Read the email and the information about the karate courses. Complete Katy's notes.

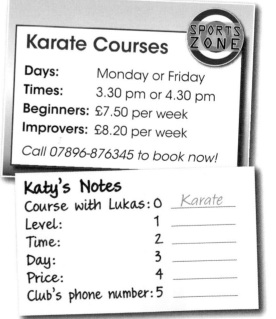

From: Lukas
To: Katy

Katy,
Thanks for asking me to do a karate course with you – what a great idea! I prefer the earlier time if that's OK with you, and Monday is not good for me because I have a tennis lesson after school that day. Of course we should do the easiest class! My phone number is 07859-567398 – call me if there is a problem.
Lukas

Karate Courses SPORTS ZONE

Days: Monday or Friday
Times: 3.30 pm or 4.30 pm
Beginners: £7.50 per week
Improvers: £8.20 per week

Call 07896-876345 to book now!

Katy's Notes
Course with Lukas: 0 *Karate*
Level: 1 _____
Time: 2 _____
Day: 3 _____
Price: 4 _____
Club's phone number: 5 _____

Exam practice: Speaking Part 2

8 Work in pairs. Student A, look at page 63. Student B, look at page 66.

9.1 It's bigger than a cat

E Reading and Writing Part 5 | **V** animals | **L** comparatives and superlatives

Vocabulary: animals

1 Write the words in the table. Can you add any more words?

| bear | camel | cat | cow | crocodile | dog | elephant |
| frog | horse | lion | monkey | parrot | sheep | tiger |

Pets	Wild animals	Farm animals

2 Read the clues and write the animals' names.

ANIMAL QUIZ

1 I'm a kind of cat, but I'm much more dangerous!   t _ _ _ _ _

2 People ride on my back and I'm good at pulling things too.   h _ _ _ _ _

3 People keep me in their homes and I sometimes work for the police.   d _ _

4 I carry luggage across the sand and I never get thirsty.   c _ _ _ _ _

5 People make sweaters from the wool that grows on my back.   s _ _ _ _ _

6 I have beautiful feathers and you can teach me to speak.   p _ _ _ _ _ _

7 I'm rather ugly, with short legs, a long tail, and lots of teeth.   c _ _ _ _ _ _ _ _

8 I'm very strong, with a thick coat and I live in mountains and forests.   b _ _ _ _

Language focus: comparatives and superlatives

3 Read the examples and complete the rules in the table.

The cat is **smaller** than the dog. The mouse is **the smallest**.
The cat is **prettier** than the dog. The mouse is **the prettiest**.
The cat is **bigger** than the mouse. The dog is **the biggest**.
The cat is **more dangerous** than the mouse.
The dog is **the most dangerous**.

1 For longer adjectives
2 For most one-syllable adjectives
3 For one-syllable adjectives that end in -y
4 For short adjectives that end with
    vowel + consonant

Comparative adjectives	Superlative adjectives
put _____ in front of the adjective	put _____ in front of the adjective
add _____ to the end	add _____ to the end
change -y to _____	change -y to _____
double the last letter and add _____	double the last letter and add _____

Irregular adjectives
good → better → the best
bad → worse → the worst

4 Compare these animals using the adjectives in the box.

beautiful	big	dangerous	dirty	fast	friendly
good	heavy	intelligent	noisy	slow	strong

0 cat / dog / sheep
1 crocodile / elephant / lion
2 camel / cow / horse
3 bear / shark / tiger
4 dolphin / mouse / monkey
5 chicken / frog / parrot

0 *A cat is friendlier than a sheep. A dog is the friendliest.*

Exam tip ✓76
Read the whole article first
to find out what it is about.

Exam practice: Reading and Writing Part 5

5 Read the article about sea lions. Choose the best word (A, B or C)
for each space.

California Sea Lions

Sea lions (0) _are_ found in the Pacific Ocean, from the north of California to Mexico. (1) _____ large animals live for up to 20 years and can (2) _____ to almost three metres long.
The (3) _____ place to see sea lions is Fisherman's Wharf in San Francisco. (4) _____ the winter there may be as many as 500 animals there, lying in the sunshine (5) _____ slowly swimming around in the water. They are very noisy too. Tourists enjoy (6) _____ them but they are less popular with fishermen because they steal their fish and break their boats.
(7) _____ is easy to teach sea lions as they are (8) _____ intelligent than many other animals. That's why there are often sea lion shows at zoos and animal parks.

0 Ⓐ are   B is   C be   5 A because   B so   C or
1 A This   B That   C These   6 A watching B watch   C watches
2 A grow   B grown   C growing   7 A There   B It   C Here
3 A good   B better C best   8 A much   B very   C more
4 A At   B During C Along

Speaking

6 Do a class survey about animals. Then tell the class what you found out.

What is the most dangerous animal?

It's going to rain

E Listening Part 1 • Reading and Writing Part 9 | **V** nature and the weather | **L** *going to* and *will*

_____'s my favourite season in my part of Japan. It often snows and it's very cold but the air is dry. We can skate on the ice on the lake and we go skiing and snowboarding in the mountains.
Akiko, Japan

I love the _____. It's starting to get warm after the long winter and there are flowers and plants and baby animals in the fields. Sometimes it gets cloudy and it rains, but afterwards the sun comes out and the countryside is fresh and green again.
Tomas, Poland

I like the bright colours of the trees in _____. They're red, orange and yellow. Sometimes it's foggy in the mornings, but the fog soon goes and the sky is blue all day long. If there's a strong wind, we can go sailing or fly our kites.
Peter, USA

_____ is my favourite time. It's very hot and sunny and I go to the beach every day to swim and play volleyball with my friends. Sometimes there are thunderstorms – they're really exciting.
Carmen, Spain

Vocabulary: nature and the weather

1 Write the seasons (*spring*, *summer*, *autumn* and *winter*) in the correct spaces above.

2 Find the things in the cartoons.

> beach __   flowers __   forest __   grass __   hills __   ice __
> island __   lake __   mountains __   plants __   sea __   trees __

3 Underline all the weather words in the cartoons and write them in the table. Can you add any more words?

Adjectives (It's...)	Verbs (It...)	Noun (There is/are a lot of...)
cold	snows	ice

A: Are you going to go to the beach this afternoon?

B: No, look at those black clouds. **It's going to rain** again.

A: Oh no! **I'll get** my raincoat. Perhaps **it'll be** sunny at the weekend.

B: I hope so. **We're going to have** a picnic on Sunday!

(104) Language focus: *going to* and *will*

4 Read the dialogue and complete the rules with *will* or *going to*.

1 We use _____ to talk about things we have decided to do in the future.
2 We use _____ to talk about things we decide to do as we are speaking.
3 We use _____ to talk about future things we are certain about.
4 We often use _____ with words like, *perhaps*, *maybe* and *probably*.

5 Ask and answer questions about the people in the cartoons. Use *going to*.

A: What's Akiko going to do?   *B: She's going to go skiing.*

6 In pairs, ask and answer questions about these times.

in 2020   in the school holidays   next year   when you leave school

A: What job will you do when you leave school?
B: I will probably be an actor.

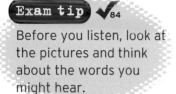

Exam tip ✔84

Before you listen, look at the pictures and think about the words you might hear.

Exam practice: Listening Part 1

🔊 20 **7** You will hear four short conversations. There is one question for each conversation. For each question, choose the right answer (A, B or C).

1 What are the man and the woman going to do today?

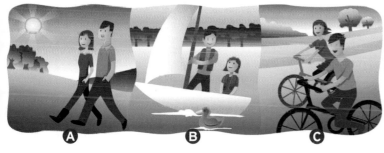

2 What will the weather be like for the skiing holiday?

3 What could the woman see from her hotel window?   4 Why is the boy late for his class?

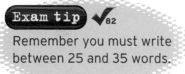

Exam tip ✔82

Remember you must write between 25 and 35 words.

Exam practice: Reading and Writing Part 9

8 Read this note from your English penfriend, Sally.

> I can't wait to visit you next month. Tell me about the area where you live. And what will the weather be like? What are we going to do together?
> Write soon,
> Sally

Write Sally an e-mail. Answer the questions. Write 25–35 words.

1 Cross out the words that don't fit.

0 Parrots / ~~Monkeys~~ / Butterflies / Penguins have wings.
1 It's **cloudy** / **fast** / **windy** / **cold** today.
2 Here's a pair of **socks** / **suit** / **shorts** / **shoes**.
3 We won the **race** / **match** / **team** / **competition**.
4 I've got a **cold** / **a temperature** / **a headache** / **an accident**.
5 Let's go **skiing** / **baseball** / **climbing** / **riding**.
6 There are **plants** / **flowers** / **trees** / **woods** growing in this garden.

2 Look at the photo. What is the article about? Make guesses with *may* and *might*.

They may be animals.
They might be dead.

3 Read the article and complete the sentences with *and*, *but*, *so*, and *when*.

0 Most people keep food in the fridge ___*but*___ Shirley Neely keeps tortoises in hers.
1 She puts the small ones in plastic boxes _____ the big ones on towels.
2 She keeps them in the fridge _____ they don't wake up during the winter.
3 Mrs Neely opens the fridge door every day _____ they get some fresh air
4 One visitor had a surprise _____ he opened the fridge door.
5 Mrs Neely will wake the tortoises up _____ the spring comes.

Close the door, we're trying to sleep!

You don't usually find living things in a fridge, but if you open Shirley Neely's two fridges you will find tortoises sleeping comfortably on every shelf. The smaller ones are packed in plastic boxes and the larger ones are covered with towels.

Mrs Neely looks after tortoises that have no homes. They sleep during the coldest months of the winter and need temperatures between 3 and 8 degrees. If it gets warmer they may wake up and then they will not be strong enough to live. 'It is easier to keep the tortoises at the correct temperature in the fridge because the weather is getting warmer nowadays. But last Saturday one of my visitors went to the fridge to get a drink. He was quite surprised!'

Before they went in the fridge the tortoises spent three weeks without food so their stomachs were empty. Then Mrs Neely bathed them and put them to bed. Everyday she opens the fridge door to check them and to let some fresh air inside. This is enough to keep the tortoises healthy. In the spring she will slowly wake them up and then she will move them into heated glasshouses in her garden.

4 Match the halves of the sentences.

0 If you open Mrs Neely's fridge...
1 Tortoises may wake up during the winter if...
2 If they wake up too soon ...
3 The tortoises sleep better if...
4 Mrs Neely opens the fridge door once a day because...
5 When winter is over, ...

A Mrs Neely starts to wake the tortoises up.
B you will get a big surprise.
C their stomachs are empty.
D it's good to let some air in.
E the temperature rises above 8 degress.
F they will probably die.

5 Give these people some advice using *you should* and *why don't you.*

0 My tooth really hurts.
(dentist) *You should go to the dentist.*

1 I lost weight and now my trousers keep falling down.
(belt) _____

2 I bought some new shoes but they are really uncomfortable.
(trainers) _____

3 I'm going to the beach tomorrow but I don't want to get sunburn.
(hat) _____

4 I want to try a new sport and meet some new friends.
(basketball) _____

5 I'm going to a party, but I don't know what to wear.
(smart shirt) _____

6 Choose the correct words to complete the sentences.

0 I really enjoy **to go /(going)** ice skating on the lake in winter.
1 I hate **to go / going** to school when it's sunny.
2 It's so windy today. I found **to walk / walking** really difficult.
3 When it rains all day, I love **to go / going** to the cinema.
4 If there is a thunderstorm tonight, I want **to stay / staying** at home.
5 Look out the window – it's starting to **snow / snowing!**

7 Make sentences using comparative and superlative adjectives.

0 a frog / a horse / an elephant (big)

A horse is bigger than a frog.
An elephant is the biggest.

1 a baseball / a football / a table tennis ball (small)
2 a hill / a mountain / a tree (tall)
3 a diamond ring / a T-shirt / a leather jacket (expensive)
4 a sheep / a crocodile / a bear (dangerous)
5 skateboarding / karate / football (easy)

On target?

How well can you do these things?	☆	☆☆	☆☆☆
E choose the correct answers to people's questions			
E choose the right words to complete a short text			
E write a short email			
V talk about clothes, sports and festivals			
V talk about nature and animals			
V talk about health and give health advice			
L use *will* and *going to* to talk about the future			
L use comparative and superlative adjectives			
L use conjunctions to join sentences together			

E **Exam skills**   V **Vocabulary skills**   L **Language skills**

10.1 What are we doing on Saturday?

E Listening Part 5 | **V** holidays | **L** present continuous for future arrangements

A

B

C

D

E

Vocabulary: holidays

1 Complete the phrases with these words.

> guide book   holiday   hotel   journey   luggage   map   ~~postcard~~
> suitcase   tickets   tour guide   tourist information office   travel agent

0 send a _postcard_
1 read a _____
2 stay at a _____
3 book your _____
4 pay the _____
5 look at a _____
6 listen to the _____
7 pack your _____
8 collect your _____
9 plan your _____
10 visit the _____
11 carry your _____

2 Which things do you do before you go on holiday? Which things do you do while you are on holiday?

3 Read the email. Are the sentences true or false?

1 Sam booked the holiday at the travel agent's.   _____
2 Sam packed his suitcase last weekend.   _____
3 Sam knows the name of the hotel.   _____
4 Sam wants to see Stella in London.   _____

To:	Stella
Subject:	Holiday

Hi Stella,
Guess what! I'm coming to London next month — without my parents! We booked the holiday over the internet last night. Mum's taking me shopping this weekend to buy a suitcase and a guide book. I'm going with a group of ten teenagers and a tour guide. We're staying in a hotel in the city centre called The Palace. Do you know it? What are you doing this summer? Are you staying in London? If you are, shall we meet up?
Write soon,
Sam

Language focus: present continuous for future arrangements

4 Read the examples and choose the correct words to complete the sentences below.

I'm coming to London next month.
Mum's taking me shopping this weekend.
What are you doing this summer?

1 These examples are about **the present** / **the future**.
2 We can use the present continuous to talk about future **arrangements** / **ideas**.
3 We usually **say** / **don't say** a future time for sentences like this.

5 Make sentences using the present continuous.

0 we / stay / in a hotel / near the beach.

We're staying in a hotel near the beach.

1 we / go / on a bus tour / tomorrow.
2 how long / we / stay / at the museum?
3 where / tour guide / take / us / today ?
4 I / buy / some postcards / for my family / later.
5 you / bring / your guide book?

Exam tip ✔90

The information in the notes and the information that you hear will be the same, but they might use different words. You need to read and listen carefully to get the right answer.

Exam practice: Listening Part 5

6 21 You will hear some information about a tour of London. Listen and complete each question.

Notes about tomorrow

Breakfast at:	(0) 8.00 a.m.
Journey to London Eye:	takes (1) _____ minutes
Price of lunch at Covent Garden:	(2) £ _____
Science Museum – name of film:	Deep (3) _____
Have dinner at the:	(4) _____
See Grease at the:	(5) _____ Theatre

Speaking

7 Work in pairs. Ask and answer questions about Sunday's tour. Student A, look at page 63. Student B, look at page 66.

> What time are we...?   What are we doing at...?
> Where are we going at... ?   How are we getting to...?

8 Work in groups. Plan a one-day tour of your area. Make a programme of things to do. Then tell other groups about your tour.

The buses are too crowded

E Listening Part 3 | **V** transport | **L** *too* and *not enough*

📁 Going to San Francisco!

Dan
UK

I'm going to San Francisco on holiday and I want to know the best way to travel around when I get there.

Louis
USA

Walk! San Francisco isn't a very big city and many of the interesting places are close together. There are lots of hills but just think how fit you will get! The buses are good but they do get very crowded. Don't even think about renting a car. The roads are difficult to drive on and it can take a long time to find a parking space because there are very few in the city.

Yu Cheng
UK

The underground, (or subway), is a great way to get around some parts of San Francisco, but it doesn't go to all the tourist areas. Walking along the waterfront is a good idea because there's so much to see, but you won't want to walk everywhere. San Francisco is a very hilly city! The famous cable cars, which are actually trams, are fun, but they cost too much to use all the time.

Anne
USA

Take the bus! There are bus stops on every corner, and if you miss one, there will be another one along soon. Walking is also a good way to get around, if you are fit enough. If you are planning to take trips outside the city, then renting a car might be a good idea, but parking spaces in the city are very expensive. The subway is good for getting to and from the airport.

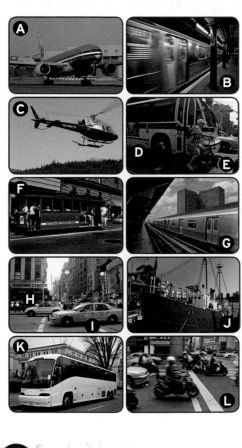

Vocabulary: transport

1 Find the modes of transport in the pictures.

bicycle ___ boat ___ bus ___ car ___ coach ___ helicopter ___ motorbike ___
plane ___ taxi ___ train ___ tram ___ the underground (the subway) ___

2 Which verbs can we use with each kind of transport?

catch   drive   fly   get on/off   get in/out of   miss   ride   sail   take

catch a bus, catch a plane

Reading

3 Read the website and answer the questions.

1 Who thinks it costs a lot of money to park your car in San Francisco?
2 Who says there are too many people on the buses?
3 Who thinks it's expensive to travel on the cable cars?
4 Who says there aren't enough parking spaces in San Francisco?
5 Who thinks the subway doesn't go to enough places?
6 Who says San Francisco is too hilly to walk everywhere?
7 Who thinks there are enough buses in San Francisco?

Language booster

too much and **too many**

We use *too much* with uncountable nouns:
too much money
too much traffic

We use *too many* with countable nouns:
too many tourists
too many cars

(105) Language focus: *too* and *not enough*

4 Read the examples and complete the rules with *too* and *not enough*.

*San Francisco is **too** expensive. It's **not** cheap **enough**!*
*The trams cost **too much** money. There are**n't enough** parking spaces.*

1 We use _____ when there is more than we want.
2 We _____ when there is less than we want.

5 Make sentences about these pictures.

0 *The window is too dirty.   The window is not clean enough.*

Exam tip ✓88

You will hear all the options for each question but only one will answer the question correctly.

Exam practice: Listening Part 3

(22) **6** Listen to Teresa talking about a trip to the US. For each question, choose the right answer (A, B or C).

0 How long did Teresa spend in the US?
  A three weeks   B four weeks   (C) six weeks
1 How did Teresa travel around while she was on holiday?
  A by bus   B by train   C by car
2 Teresa's parents thought Disneyland was too
  A crowded.   B expensive.   C big.
3 What did Teresa do at the Grand Canyon?
  A went for a walk   B took a ride in a helicopter   C went on a plane
4 Teresa and her family did not visit
  A Los Angeles.   B Las Vegas.   C Phoenix.
5 What did Teresa's mother enjoy most in San Francisco?
  A the bridge   B the food   C the zoo

Speaking

7 Imagine some friends are visiting your area and want to know about travelling around. Think of some advice to give them.

Taxis are too expensive. You should take the bus.

11.1 Have you been there?

E Listening Part 4 • Reading and Writing Part 4 | **V** buildings | **L** present perfect versus past simple

cinema / stadium / museum

motorway / bridge / crossroads

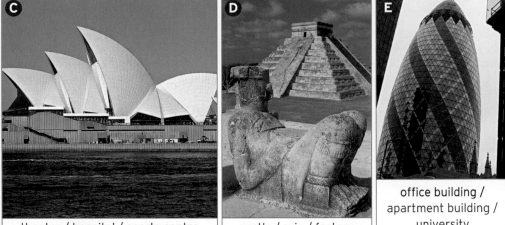

theatre / hospital / sports centre

castle / ruin / factory

office building /
apartment building /
university

Vocabulary: buildings

1 Look at the photos and decide what kind of buildings they are. Do you know the names of the buildings? Where are they?

Exam practice: Listening Part 4

2 You will hear a girl asking about things to do in a town called Hadley. Listen and complete each question.

> **Hadley**
> Castle built in: (0) _13th century_
> Swimming pool in: (1) _____
> Name of this week's film: (2) The Tale of _____
> Cinema tickets on weekdays cost: (3) £ _____
> Skatepark: opposite the   (4) _____
> Post Office closes at: (5) _____

Language booster

just, yet and *already*

Use *just* with actions that happened not long ago:
*She's **just** bought some stamps.*

Use *already* with actions that are completed:
*She's **already** bought some stamps.*

Use *yet* with actions that are not completed:
*She hasn't bought any stamps **yet**.*

Language focus: present perfect versus past simple

3 Read the examples and choose the correct words to complete the rules.

*Tina **went** to the swimming pool last week.*
*Tina **has been** to the cinema, but she's **never been** to the skatepark.*
*Liz **has been** in England **since** Monday.*
*Tina **has lived** in Hadley **for** ten years.*

1 We use the *past simple / present perfect* when we are talking about the day or time that something happened.
2 We use the *past simple / present perfect* when we are talking about something that happened in the past, but we are not saying when it happened.
3 We also use the present perfect with *for* or *since* to talk about things that started in the past and are not finished. We use *for / since* with times, days and dates, and we use *for / since* to say how long.

post office / railway station / castle

bank / church / library

4 Complete the dialogues using the present perfect or the past simple.

1 A: _____ (you / go to) the cinema last night?
   B: No, _____ (I / go) there on Friday.
2 A: _____ (you / ever / visit) Liverpool?
   B: Yes, _____ (I / go) there two years ago.
3 A: _____ (you / arrive) on Saturday?
   B: No, _____ (I / be) here since Wednesday.
4 A: _____ (you / see) the bridge yesterday?
   B: No, _____ (I / no / see) yet.

Exam practice: Reading and Writing Part 4

5 Read this page from a guide book about Liverpool. Are sentences 1–7 'Right' (A) or 'Wrong' (B)? If there is not enough information to answer 'Right' (A) or 'Wrong' (B), choose 'Doesn't say' (C).

The Albert Dock

Liverpool's Albert Dock, a short walk from the city centre, has small shops, museums, clubs and cafés where you can sit and watch the activity on the river.
The Albert Dock was built in 1846, when Liverpool was a busy port, with big ships bringing goods from all over the world, but by the 1950s the dock was used very little. For over 20 years now it has been very popular with tourists.

Things to do

The Maritime Museum tells the story of the men who once worked on the big ships. In this big 19th-century dock building, visitors can also learn about the many people who sailed from Liverpool to look for a better life in other countries. There are also rooms full of beautiful furniture from the ships that carried rich passengers to New York.

Next door, Tate Liverpool has many important works of 20th-century art. The entrance hall of this fine old building has now become an area for smaller exhibitions. The amazing Yellow Duckmarine is a bus that visits some of the interesting places along the river before driving down into the river at the Albert Dock. You've never done anything like this before!

0 It is easy to reach the Albert Dock on foot from the city centre. (A) B C
1 Tourists have enjoyed coming to the Albert Dock since 1846.   A B C
2 The Maritime Museum is in a new building.   A B C
3 The people who moved to other countries found their
   lives improved.   A B C
4 You can see modern art in Tate Liverpool.   A B C
5 The exhibitions in the entrance hall of Tate Liverpool
   often change.   A B C
6 Passengers can get on and off the Yellow Duckmarine
   during the tour.   A B C
7 The Yellow Duckmarine travels on roads and in the water.   A B C

Speaking

6 Ask and answer questions about places your partner has visited.

another country	an unusual art gallery	a famous building
an interesting museum	a famous place	a terrible restaurant
a very quiet place	a very old building	

A: *Have you ever been to the UK?*
B: *Yes, I have. I went there in 2007.*
A: *Which cities did you go to?*

Turn left at the traffic lights

E Reading and Writing Part 1 and Part 7 | **V** places in town | **L** giving directions

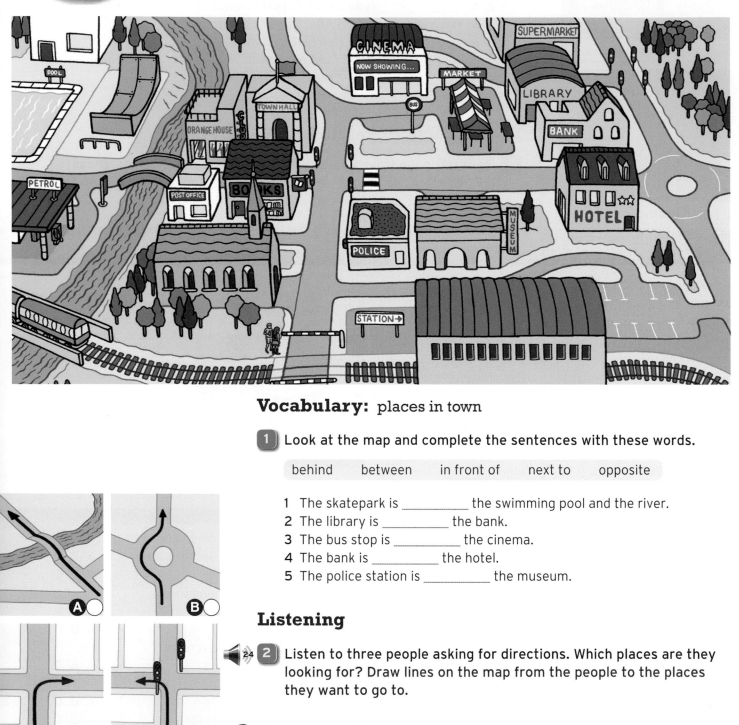

Vocabulary: places in town

1 Look at the map and complete the sentences with these words.

> behind   between   in front of   next to   opposite

1 The skatepark is _____ the swimming pool and the river.
2 The library is _____ the bank.
3 The bus stop is _____ the cinema.
4 The bank is _____ the hotel.
5 The police station is _____ the museum.

Listening

24 **2** Listen to three people asking for directions. Which places are they looking for? Draw lines on the map from the people to the places they want to go to.

106 ## Language focus: giving directions

3 Match the directions to the pictures.

1 Turn left at the traffic lights.
2 Turn right at the crossroads.
3 Go straight on at the roundabout.
4 Take the second road on the right.
5 Go over the bridge.
6 Go past the library.

4 Work in pairs. Help your partner find some places on your map. Student A, look at page 64. Student B, look at page 67.

How do I get to the museum?

Exam practice: Reading and Writing Part 1

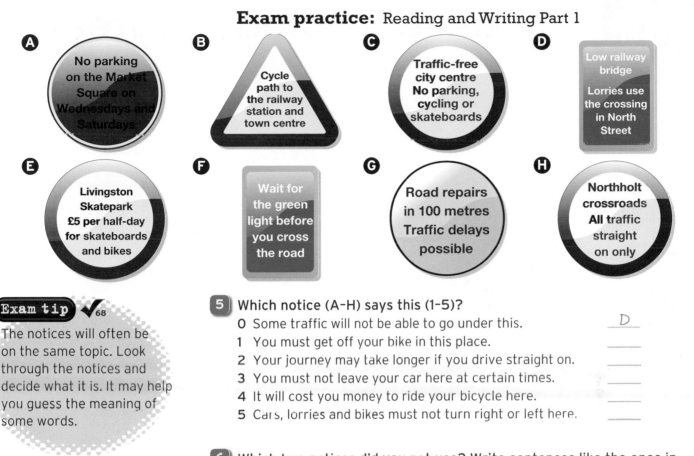

A No parking on the Market Square on Wednesdays and Saturdays

B Cycle path to the railway station and town centre

C Traffic-free city centre No parking, cycling or skateboards

D Low railway bridge Lorries use the crossing in North Street

E Livingston Skatepark £5 per half-day for skateboards and bikes

F Wait for the green light before you cross the road

G Road repairs in 100 metres Traffic delays possible

H Northholt crossroads All traffic straight on only

Exam tip ✔68

The notices will often be on the same topic. Look through the notices and decide what it is. It may help you guess the meaning of some words.

5 Which notice (A–H) says this (1–5)?

0 Some traffic will not be able to go under this.   _D_
1 You must get off your bike in this place.   _____
2 Your journey may take longer if you drive straight on.   _____
3 You must not leave your car here at certain times.   _____
4 It will cost you money to ride your bicycle here.   _____
5 Cars, lorries and bikes must not turn right or left here.   _____

6 Which two notices did you not use? Write sentences like the ones in Activity 5 to explain what they mean.

Exam practice: Reading and Writing Part 7

7 Complete these emails. Write ONE word for each space.

Exam tip ✔79

Remember you must only write ONE word in the space and it must be spelled correctly.

From: Luis
To: Jake

Hi Jake,
I (0) _have_ decided to come on the 1.15 train on Saturday. Will you meet me (1) _____ the station?
Luis

From: Jake
To: Luis

Hi Luis
My teacher has asked me (2) _____ play in a football match and I won't be home (3) _____ 3.30. Sorry! But it's easy to find my house and Mum and Dad will be (4) _____. When you (5) _____ off the train walk through the car park and then go (6) _____ on. At the end (7) _____ right and cross the road. My house is number 14. You can't miss (8) _____. If you go (9) _____ the church you have gone (10) _____ far!
Jake

Speaking

8 Think of a place in your town. Tell your classmates how to get there from your school. Who can guess the place first?

First go out of the main doors and turn right. Then go straight on...

I think technology is great

E Reading and Writing Part 5 | **V** technology | **L** *believe, hope, know, say* and *think*

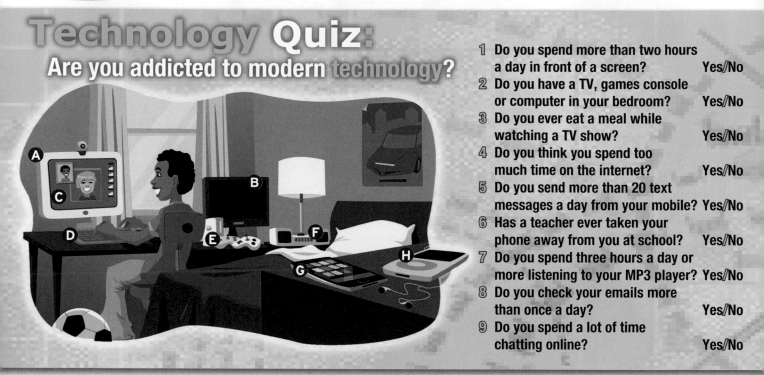

Technology Quiz:
Are you addicted to modern technology?

1 Do you spend more than two hours a day in front of a screen? Yes/No
2 Do you have a TV, games console or computer in your bedroom? Yes/No
3 Do you ever eat a meal while watching a TV show? Yes/No
4 Do you think you spend too much time on the internet? Yes/No
5 Do you send more than 20 text messages a day from your mobile? Yes/No
6 Has a teacher ever taken your phone away from you at school? Yes/No
7 Do you spend three hours a day or more listening to your MP3 player? Yes/No
8 Do you check your emails more than once a day? Yes/No
9 Do you spend a lot of time chatting online? Yes/No

Vocabulary: technology

1 Find the technology items in the picture.

computer __   games console __   keyboard __   mobile phone __
MP3 player __   radio __   screen __   television __

2 Use these words to make silly sentences about the things in the picture. Can you correct your partner's sentences?

Actions
chat to   listen to   play
record   send   surf   type
watch   visit

Things
cartoons   emails   friends
the internet   music
programmes   websites

A: You use an MP3 player to type emails.
B: No, you don't. You use an MP3 player to listen to music.

3 Try the technology quiz. Then check the results on page 64.

Listening

25 **4** You will hear a teenager called Annie speaking on a radio phone-in programme. Listen and answer the questions.

1 How long does Annie spend online every day?
2 How many text messages does she send every day?
3 When did the teacher take her phone away from her?
4 Does Annie think modern technology is bad for teens?

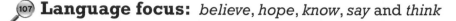

Language focus: *believe, hope, know, say* and *think*

5 Read the examples and choose the correct words to complete the rules.

*Some parents **believe** (that) technology is bad for their children.*
*My mum **says** (that) I use too much technology.*
*I don't **think** (that) 60 messages is a lot.*
*I **hope** (that) you weren't sending text messages in class.*
*Yeah, I **know** (that) I shouldn't use my phone in class.*

1 We **have to / don't have to** use *that* after these words.
2 We **often use / never use** the continuous forms of *believe* and *know*.

6 Match the two halves of the sentences.

1 Annie says (that) she...
2 Annie hopes (that) she...
3 Annie knows (that) she...
4 Annie thinks (that) it...
5 Annie doesn't think (that) adults...
6 Annie believes (that) modern technology...

A is possible to study and send text messages at the same time.
B spends two hours a day online.
C should worry so much about teenagers.
D will get her phone back soon.
E is good for teenagers.
F shouldn't use her phone in class.

Exam tip

Read the text through once before choosing the words for the spaces.

Exam practice: Reading and Writing Part 5

7 Read the article about a girl who won a prize. Choose the best word (A, B or C) for each space.

The $25,000 Text Message

In April 2007, Morgan Pozgar became the first (0) _____ National Texting Champion of the United States. She won the competition in New York (1) _____ typing a message of 151 letters in 42 seconds. She beat 250 (2) _____ people to win the top prize of $25,000. Morgan, (3) _____ was thirteen years old at the time, sends (4) _____ than 7,000 text messages a month.

In the final she beat a 21-year-old girl called Eli Tirosh. Eli finished first and everyone (5) _____ that she was the winner. But then the judges found a mistake in (6) _____ text message, and said that Morgan was the winner.

The phone used in the competition had a QWERTY keyboard, so it was (7) _____ to use than a normal mobile phone. (8) _____ she won, Morgan said, "I can't believe that I actually won the whole competition. Now I want to go shopping!"

0 (A) ever	B only	C yet		5 A thinks	B thinking	C thought
1 A at	B by	C to		6 A its	B her	C their
2 A such	B each	C other		7 A easy	B easier	C easiest
3 A what	B which	C who		8 A When	B If	C While
4 A more	B much	C most				

Speaking

8 Do a short survey about technology. Ask questions about some of these topics: computers, mobile phones, television, video games.

Do you think video games are bad for young children?

Vocabulary: books and reading

1 Match the words to the things in the picture.

comic __   dictionary __   magazine __   newspaper __   novel __

2 Where can you find the things in the box? Use the words from Activity 1.

advertisement   article   cartoon   crossword   information about a place or person   information about a word   photograph   picture   sports news   exciting story   weather report

Exam Practice: Speaking Part 2

3 Work in pairs. Student A, look at page 65. Student B, look at page 67.

🔍 107 Language focus: past continuous

4 Read the examples and look at the diagram. Which verb is A and which is B?

1 Claudia **was reading** a comic when the teacher **walked in**.
2 When the teacher **walked in**, Paula **was sitting** in her chair.

A ■————————————|————————————■ B

5 Choose the correct words to complete the rule.

We make the past continuous with the past of **to be** / **to do** and the **-ing** / **-ed** form of the verb.

Language booster

when and *while*

Use *when* before the past simple:
When she walked in, I was sleeping.

Use *while* before the past continuous:
She walked in while I was sleeping.

What was Claudia doing when the teacher walked in?

She was reading a comic.

6 Ask and answer questions about the people in the picture.

7 Tell your partner what you were doing yesterday at these times. Make true and false sentences. Are your partner's sentences true?

8.00 a.m.   9.30 a.m.   1.00 p.m.   4.00 p.m.   8.00 p.m.   11.00 p.m.

A: At 1.00 p.m. I was eating a hot dog.
B: No, you weren't! You always have sandwiches for lunch.

Exam practice: Reading and Writing Part 4

8 Read the article below. Who is the story about? What happened? Where did it happen?

9 Read the article again. Are sentences 1–7 'Right' (A) or 'Wrong' (B)? If there is not enough information to answer 'Right' (A) or 'Wrong' (B), choose 'Doesn't Say' (C).

A Teenage Heroine

Police in Australia say that they want to give sixteen-year-old Laura Simpson an award for bravery because she saved the lives of 38 passengers on a bus. Laura was travelling home from her boarding school when suddenly the bus turned off the road. "It was 3.00 a.m., so I was sleeping," Laura said, "but then I felt a big bump and woke up. The bus was off the road and going towards the trees. I looked at the driver and saw he was lying over the wheel and his lips were blue. He wasn't moving. I jumped out of my seat and took the wheel. I shouted for someone to call an ambulance." Laura then stopped the bus, found a torch, and helped the other passengers off the bus.

After the ambulance left, Laura phoned the bus company and asked for a new driver. He didn't arrive until the next day. While they were waiting for him, she and some of the other passengers played football and sang songs.

Laura's story has been in all the newspapers and on TV. "Someone even rang me from Scotland! I can't believe how far it has gone!" she said. Laura plans to spend her school holiday helping her parents on their farm and learning to drive. "I hope I pass my test!" she said.

Exam tip ✓74

If you cannot find any information about a question, choose C.

0 The Australian police think Laura should get a prize.   Ⓐ B C
1 Laura was on her way to school when the accident happened.   A B C
2 All the passengers on the bus were students at Laura's school.   A B C
3 When Laura woke up she saw that the driver was ill.   A B C
4 Another passenger helped Laura to stop the bus.   A B C
5 When the new bus driver arrived some of the passengers were listening to music.   A B C
6 Laura is surprised that people in different countries have heard her story.   A B C
7 Laura already has a driving licence.   A B C

Writing

10 In pairs, write a story about meeting a famous person. Use this plan to help you. Then read your story to the class. Which is the best story?

Beginning: Where were you? What were you doing?
Middle: Which famous person did you see? What was he or she doing?
End: What did you say? What did the famous person say?

It was a sunny day, so I went to the park...

Review 4

1 Which word is the odd one out?

0 happy busy (long) friendly
1 boring funny interesting excellent
2 television radio newspaper chat
3 traffic lights market crossing roundabout
4 bookshop supermarket newsagent bank
5 wheel bus train bicycle
6 walk fly drive ticket
7 keyboard screen mouse click
8 online internet website favourite

2 Complete the mini-dialogues.

0 A: Where are my sunglasses?

   B: *They're next to the lamp.*

1 A: Where is my mobile phone?

   B: _____

2 A: Have you seen my dictionary?

   B: _____

3 A: I can't find my mp3 player. Where is it?

   B: _____

4 A: Where's my comic?

   B: _____

5 A: Have you seen my keyboard?

   B: _____

3 Write about Victoria's plans for this week.

Monday: cinema with Boris
Tuesday: meet Debbie at museum
Wednesday: get money from bank
Thursday: borrow a guidebook from library
Friday: buy tickets from railway station
Saturday: go to Paris

On Monday, she's going to the cinema with Boris.

4 Complete the sentences about David's travel experiences.

0 David *has not ridden* (**not ride**) a bicycle around the world.

1 David _____ (**take**) a train across Russia.

2 David _____ (**use**) the underground trains in London.

3 David _____ (**not fly**) in a helicopter.

4 David _____ (**not drive**) a bus in New York.

5 David _____ (**sail**) a boat from England to France.

5 Complete the dialogues with *too* or *not enough*.

0 A: Is there a bank near here?
   B: Yes, just go straight on down this road. It's not ___*too far*___ (**far**).

1 A: Should I take the bus or the train?
   B: Take the train. The bus is _____ (**slow**).

2 A: Do you want to go to the castle?
   B: No, it's _____ (**late**) now. Let's go tomorrow.

3 A: Is the museum here good?
   B: It's OK, but it's _____ (**big**). It only takes an hour to see everything.

4 A: Should I turn right here to get to the castle?
   B: No, it's _____ (**soon**). Take the next right.

5 A: Where are we?
   B: I don't know! This map is _____ (**good**).

6 Make sentences using the prompts.

0 Sam: "I like listening to music."
he / says / likes / music / to / Sam / listening / .

Sam says he likes listening to music.

1 Claudia: "I want to make my own website this year."
this year / hopes / to / website / make / own / her / Claudia / .

_____

2 Viktor: "I think that we won't use keyboards in the future."
future / the / keyboards / use / people / won't / believes / Viktor / in / .

_____

3 Lorretta: "I chat to my friends online every day."
she / says / every / day / uses / Loretta / chatrooms / .

_____

4 Cassandra: "I spend too much time surfing the internet."
knows / too / much / spends / time / online / Cassandra / she /.

_____

5 Jun: "Typing emails is boring. It's easier to phone my friends."
phoning / people / Jun / emailing / thinks / better / is / them / than / .

_____

7 Look at the pictures and make sentences. Use the past continuous and the past simple with *when* or *because*.

0 _I was doing my homework when I fell asleep._

On target?

How well can you do these things?	☆	☆☆	☆☆☆
E listen for key information			
E read for detailed understanding			
E use grammar knowledge to complete a short text			
V talk about technology			
V talk about travel and holidays			
V talk about my town and give directions			
L use the past continous to tell a story			
L make complaints with *too* and *not enough*			
L use the present perfect to talk about experiences			

E Exam skills   V Vocabulary skills   L Language skills

Pairwork activities

Unit 1 Lesson 2: Student A

3 Ask and answer the questions in pairs to complete Sue's timetable.

*What does Sue study **at** ten forty-five **on** Monday?   She studies...*

	Monday	Tuesday	Wednesday	Thursday	Friday
9.10	Maths		History	English	
9.50	Design	English			Maths
10.30	**BREAK**				
10.45		Maths	French	Geography	Science
11.25	Art	Science	Music	Science	Drama
12.05	**LUNCH**				
1.15	Science		English	History	Geography
1.55	History	Sport	Maths		Design
2.35	Computer Studies	Sport		French	Art
3.15	**GO HOME**				

Unit 3 Lesson 2: Student A

2 1 Here is some information about a party. Student B does not know anything about the party, so he/she will ask you some questions about it.

2 Student B has some information about a shop. You don't know anything about the shop. Use the question prompts to ask Student B about the shop.

LET'S PARTY!

Veronika's 13th Birthday Party!

at Club Starlight

on Saturday 10th June
from 8 pm – 11 pm
No jeans or T-shirts
Reply to: *veronika@compco.net*

PARTY SHOP

• name of the shop?
• address?
• when / open?
• website?
• what / sell?

Unit 8 Lesson 1: Student A

7 1 Tell your partner about these health problems. Your partner will give you some advice.

   A I feel tired all the time.
   B I can't fall asleep at night.
   C I've got a pain in my back.

   2 Now your partner will tell you about some health problems. Listen and say what the problem might be. Then give some advice.

Unit 8 Lesson 2: Student A

8 1 Here is some information about some swimming lessons. Answer B's questions about the swimming lessons.

2 Student B has some information about a football match. You don't know anything about the football match so ask B some questions about it.

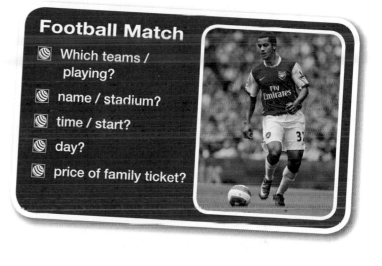

Unit 10 Lesson 1: Student A

7 You have half of the group's programme. Student B has the other half. Ask and answer questions to complete the programme.

Sunday's Programme
9.30	have breakfast
10.30	visit the Tower of London
1.00	
2.00	travel to the Houses of Parliament and Big Ben
	by _____
4.30	visit _____
6.00	return to hotel
	leave the hotel
8.00	have dinner at _____

Unit 11 Lesson 2: Student A

4 1 Ask Student B for directions to these places and mark them on your map.

A the museum   B the market place   C the post office

2 Look at your map and answer Student B's questions.

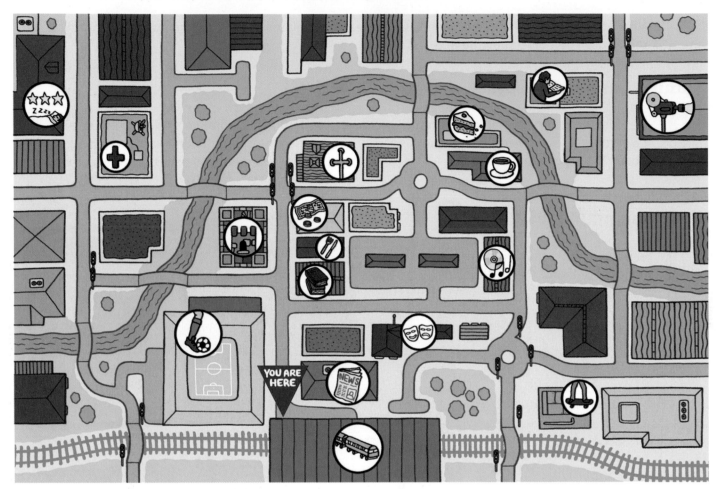

Unit 12 Lesson 1

3

RESULTS
How many questions did you answer with 'yes'?

0 – 3: You are not addicted to modern technology at all. In fact, you think spending time with real people is more important than watching TV or playing computer games. A great result!

4 – 6: You do not have a problem yet but you need to be careful. Try to spend more time on your hobbies, and less time in front of a screen. You probably don't believe it, but you will feel much better.

7 – 9: Oh dear! You are addicted to modern technology. Why don't you switch everything off for a week and see what happens? You may be surprised at how much fun life can be without these things!

Unit 12 Lesson 2: Student A

3 1 Here is some information about a magazine for teens. Answer B's questions about the magazine.

2 You don't know anything about the library so ask B some questions about it.

YOUR WORLD

A new magazine for teens!

On sale every month
Stories, photos and news.
Only £2.50
Buy it in all good newsagents

Hilden Library

- computers ?
- address ?
- get / coffee ?
- books for teenagers ?
- open / every day ?

Unit 1 Lesson 2: Student B

3 Ask and answer the questions in pairs to complete Sue's timetable.

What does Sue study at ten past nine on Wednesday? She studies...

	Monday	Tuesday	Wednesday	Thursday	Friday
9.10	Maths	French		English	Computer Studies
9.50	Design	English	Science	Music	Maths
10.30	**BREAK**				
10.45	English	Maths	French		Science
11.25		Science		Science	
12.05	**LUNCH**				
1.15	Science	Geography	English	History	Geography
1.55	History		Maths	Maths	
2.35	Computer Studies		Drama	French	Art
3.15	**GO HOME**				

Unit 3 Lesson 2: Student B

2 1 Student A has some information about a party. You don't know anything about the party. Use the question prompts to ask Student B about the party.

2 Here is some information about a shop. Student B doesn't know anything about the shop, so he/she will ask you some questions about it.

PARTY

- whose?
- how old?
- where?
- time?
- wear?

FAB FUN

Everything you need for your party!
- cards
- balloons
- invitations
- paper plates and cups

25 Kings Road

Open daily 9 am — 5 pm

www.fabfun.co.uk

Unit 8 Lesson 1: Student B

7 1 Your partner will tell you about some health problems. Listen and say what the problem might be. Then give some advice.

2 Now tell your partner about these health problems. Your partner will give you some advice.

A I'm not very fit.
B I've cut my hand.
C My eyes hurt when I use the computer.

Unit 8 Lesson 2: Student B

8 1 Student A has some information about some swimming lessons. You don't know anything about the swimming lessons so ask A some questions about them.

2 Here is some information about a football match. Answer A's questions about the football match.

Swimming lessons

- name / pool?
- for children?
- lessons / Saturday?
- expensive?
- address?

Football Match!

Arsenal v Barnet
City Stadium
Saturday 25th June
Family ticket – £25.00
Match starts at 3.00 pm

Unit 10 Lesson 1: Student B

7 You have half of the group's programme. Student A has the other half. Ask and answer questions to complete the programme.

Sunday's Programme

9.30	
10.30	visit the _____
1.00	have a picnic lunch
2.00	take a boat to the _____
4.30	visit Westminster Abbey
	return to hotel
7.30	leave the hotel
8.00	_____ at the Hard Rock Café

Unit 11 Lesson 2: Student B

4 1 Look at the map and answer Student A's questions.

2 Ask Student A for directions to these places and mark them on your map.

    A the hotel   **B** the cinema   **C** the skatepark

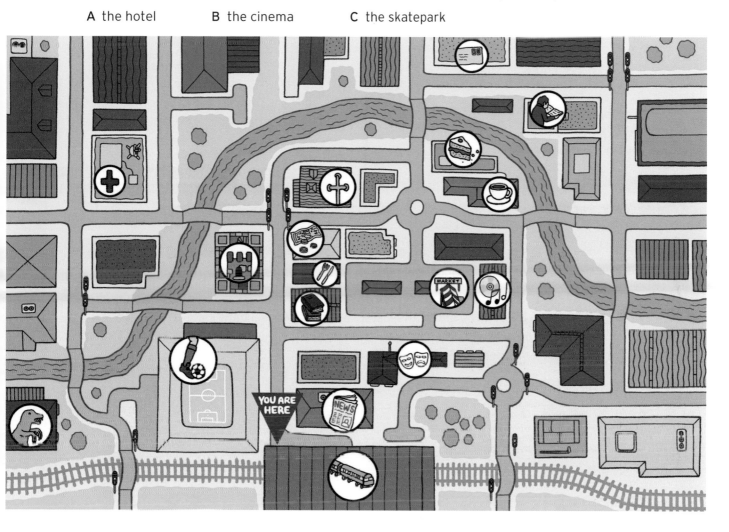

Unit 12 Lesson 2: Student B

3 1 Here is some information about a library. Answer A's questions about the library.

2 You don't know anything about the magazine so ask A some questions about it.

Hilden Library

22 Park Street
Books for children, teenagers
and adults
5 new computers
Open Monday to Saturday 9.00-6.00
Coffee machine

New Magazine

- name ?
- magazine / £ ?
- what / inside ?
- when / buy it ?
- where / buy it ?

Exam guide ✔

General Tips

When you do KET, you will get a question paper and an answer sheet.

This is a question paper:

This is an answer sheet:

KEY ENGLISH TEST for Schools

PAPER 1   Reading and Writing

Time   1 hour 10 minutes

Examination Title

Centre

Supervisor:
If the candidate is ABSENT or has WITHDRAWN shade here

KET Paper 1 Reading and Writing Candidate Answer Sheet

Instructions

You can make notes on the question paper. For example, you can make notes while you listen, or you can underline parts of the reading texts.

You must write your answers on the answer sheet, so make sure you leave enough time to do this. At the end of the Listening paper you will have eight minutes to transfer your answers to the answer sheets, but there is no extra time for the Reading and Writing paper.

For some questions, you need to put a mark below a letter, like this:

- Fill in your answers carefully and rub out any mistakes.
- Only choose one answer.

For some questions, you need to write a word, like this:

- Write your answers clearly, so the examiner can easily read them.
- Check your spelling.

Reading and Writing • Part 1

What do I have to do?

- You need to match each sentence to the notice with the same meaning.
- There are five sentences (1–5) and an example (O).
- There are eight notices (A–H), so there are two that you will not use.

How do I do it?

- All the notices might be about the same topic, so you might be able to use the topic to help you guess the meanings of words you don't know.
- Find the important words in the question. Then look for words with similar meanings in the notices.
- Think about the meaning of the notices. You shouldn't choose a notice just because it uses the same word or number as the question.
- Remember, you can't use the notice that was used in the example.

Over to you

Questions 1–5

Which notice (**A–H**) says this (**1–5**)?
For questions **1–5**, mark the correct letter **A–H** on your answer sheet.

Example:	*Answer:*	**0**	A B C D E F G H

0	Go here if you are thirsty.	**A**	**Please leave this picnic area clean and tidy**
1	This place is only for walkers.	**B**	Come and see the dolphins! Shows daily 2 pm and 4 pm
2	You can go here to watch something every afternoon.	**C**	**Entrance — Children's zoo** Please shut the gate behind you
3	Children and adults can get something to ride here.	**D**	**Public footpath** **No horses, bicycles or motorbikes**
4	You cannot sleep in a tent here.	**E**	**CAMPSITE OPEN** **1ST MAY – 30TH SEPTEMBER**
5	You must not leave this open.	**F**	**DURSLEY WOODS** **NO OVERNIGHT CAMPING OR FIRES**
		G	**Beach Café** We sell ice creams, snacks and drinks
		H	**Bicycles to rent** all ages and sizes

Reading and Writing • Part 2

What do I have to do?

- There are five sentences (6-10) and an example (0).
- All the sentences are about the same topic and they may also tell a story.
- You need to choose the correct words to complete the sentences.
- There are three words to choose from (A, B or C).
- This part of the exam tests your knowledge of vocabulary.

How do I do it?

- First read the instructions to find out the topic.
- Next read through all the sentences to get the basic meaning.
- Read the whole sentence before you choose your answer.
- Try all three options in the space before you choose your answer.
- Choose carefully because the three words are similar, but are used in different ways.
- You may need to think about grammar to choose the correct word.

Over to you

Questions 6–10

Read the sentences about going to a restaurant.
Choose the best word (**A**, **B** or **C**) for each space.
For questions **6–10**, mark **A**, **B** or **C** on your answer sheet.

Example:

0	It was Ron's birthday and his parents .... him what he wanted to do.				
	A asked	**B** talked	**C** spoke	*Answer:*	0 A■ B☐ C☐

---

6   Ron wanted to go to a restaurant for a .... with some friends.

    A   meal   **B**   plate   **C**   food

7   He .... a restaurant near the centre of town called 'The Silver Fish'.

    A   thought   **B** decided   **C**   chose

8   'The Silver Fish' is the most .... restaurant in town.

    A   favourite   **B**   popular   **C**   nice

9   His parents were happy because it doesn't .... much to eat there.

    A   cost   **B**   pay   **C**   spend

10   They spent a long .... in the restaurant and had lots of fun.

    A   hour   **B**   time   **C**   moment

Reading and Writing • Part 3 (a)

What do I have to do?

- You need to complete some short conversations.
- There are five conversations (11-15) and an example (0).
- You need to read what the first person says and choose what the other person says.
- The first person might ask a question or say a sentence.
- There are three possible answers to choose from (A, B or C).

How do I do it?

- First read what the first person says and think about when or where you might say it.
- Think of some possible answers.
- Look at the three possible replies. Don't just choose a reply because it looks similar or uses the same words.
- Think carefully about the meaning of each answer and choose the best one.

Over to you

Questions 11–15

Complete the five conversations.
For questions **11–15**, mark **A**, **B** or **C** on your answer sheet.

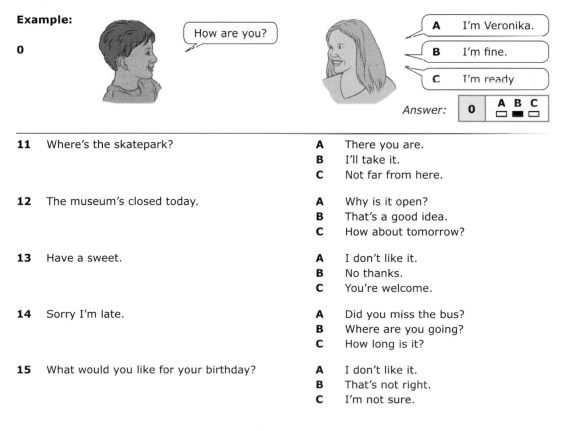

Example:

0   How are you?

  A   I'm Veronika.
  B   I'm fine.
  C   I'm ready

Answer: 0   A B C (B marked)

11	Where's the skatepark?	A	There you are.
		B	I'll take it.
		C	Not far from here.

12	The museum's closed today.	A	Why is it open?
		B	That's a good idea.
		C	How about tomorrow?

13	Have a sweet.	A	I don't like it.
		B	No thanks.
		C	You're welcome.

14	Sorry I'm late.	A	Did you miss the bus?
		B	Where are you going?
		C	How long is it?

15	What would you like for your birthday?	A	I don't like it.
		B	That's not right.
		C	I'm not sure.

Reading and Writing • Part 3 (b)

What do I have to do?

- You need to complete a conversation.
- You can see what one speaker says.
- You need to choose the things that the other speaker says.
- There are five spaces to fill (16-20) and an example at the beginning (0).
- There is a list of eight options (A-H) that you can use to complete the conversation, so there are two that you will not use.

How do I do it?

- First read the instructions to find out who the people are.
- Read the conversation to find out what the people are talking about.
- Read all the options (A-H) you can add.
- Think about what comes before and after the space to choose the correct answer.
- You may need to think about grammar when you choose your answer.
- After you have finished, read the whole conversation again to check your answers.

Exam Extra!

Yes and No

There are lots of different ways of saying *yes* and *no*.

Look at the phrases below. Write *Y* for phrases that mean *yes*.
Write *N* for phrases that mean *no*.

_____ Sure.	_____ Certainly.
_____ Never!	_____ OK.
_____ I'm afraid not.	_____ Of course.
_____ I'd love to.	_____ I'm sorry, I can't.
_____ That's right.	_____ Fine.

Over to you

Questions 16–20

Complete the conversation between two friends.
What does Matt say to Andy?
For questions **16–20**, mark the correct letter **A–H** on your answer sheet.

Example:

Andy: Hi, Matt. What are you doing this evening?

Matt: **0** ....D......

Answer:

0	A	B	C	D	E	F	G	H
	☐	☐	☐	■	☐	☐	☐	☐

Andy: Well, the manager of my football team is looking for new players.

Matt: **16** ....

Andy: You are! Anyway, just come and try! It's good fun.

Matt: **17** ....

Andy: That's right, at 4.00 p.m., after class.

Matt: **18** ....

Andy: You're a size 41, aren't you? I've got a pair you can wear.

Matt: **19** ....

Andy: They're in the changing room, so let's meet there at 3.45.

Matt: **20** ....

Andy: Good idea! See you later.

A   I hope trainers will be OK. I haven't got any football boots.

B   Fine. Shall I ask James to come as well? He loves football.

C   Oh, that sounds interesting. But I don't think I'm good enough.

D   Not much, Andy. Why?

E   Thanks, Andy. Shall I come and get them now?

F   What time does it start?

G   OK, I will. You play on the school field, don't you?

H   Do I need to wear anything special?

Reading and Writing • Part 4

What do I have to do?

- You need to read a newspaper article or part of a book and answer some questions.
- There are seven questions (21–27) and an example (0).
- There are three task types for Reading and Writing Part 4:

Multiple choice

- You need to read a text and choose the answers to the questions.

0   The biggest street festival in the world is in

A   London.   **B**   Germany.   **C**   Rio.

Matching

- You read three texts about three similar things. For example, they might be about three books, three people, or three films.
- You need to decide which of the three things is the answer to each question.

0   Who decided to be an actor at a very early age?

A   Emma   **B**   Daniel   **C**   Rupert

Right / Wrong / Doesn't say

- You need to read a text and say if some sentences are right, wrong, or if there is not enough information to decide.

0   Jay Shafer's house has everything except a bathroom.

A   Right   **B**   Wrong   **C**   Doesn't say

How do I do it?

- Read the instructions. They will tell you what the text is about. There might be a picture to help you too.
- Read the article. You should try to get the basic meaning of the article, so don't worry if there are any words you don't understand.
- Read the questions. They are in the same order as the information in the text.
- Find the part of the text that has the information you need to answer each question and read it again carefully.
- Remember, the words in the text and the question may look the same, but the meaning may be different.
- If you are doing a **Right / Wrong / Doesn't say** question, remember the information you are looking for might not be there. If you can't find anything, choose **C** (Doesn't say).

Over to you

Questions 21–27

Read the article about a young man who works on aeroplanes.
Are sentences **21–27** 'Right' **(A)** or 'Wrong' **(B)**?
If there is not enough information to answer 'Right' **(A)** or 'Wrong' **(B)**, choose 'Doesn't say' **(C)**.
For questions **21–27**, mark **A**, **B** or **C** on your answer sheet.

Ryan MacMahon – flight attendant

'I've always loved aeroplanes. When I was child my grandfather often took me to Manchester Airport to watch the planes. Then, for my sixteenth birthday, my parents paid for me to have a flying lesson in a single-engine plane. It was fantastic!

I've been a flight attendant for two years now. I really enjoy looking after the passengers: talking to them and checking that they are safe and comfortable. They are all so different and interesting; I am always learning something new. I love the feeling of being in the air. I like it best when there's a storm and we have to tell the passengers to put on their seat belts.

My favourite flight is the night flight from London to Tenerife. We fly down the west coast of Portugal and you can see the lights of the big cities in the water, like a mirror. I'm lucky to work for this company, because we never have to pay for our flights when we go on holiday. I've had holidays all over the world, but I like Timanfaya National Park in Lanzarote best – it's like being on the moon.'

Example:

0 Ryan went alone to watch planes at the airport when he was young.

    A Right   **B** Wrong   **C** Doesn't say   *Answer:*

0	A	B	C
	☐	■	☐

---

21 When Ryan was a teenager his parents taught him to fly.

    A Right   **B** Wrong   **C** Doesn't say

22 Ryan started working as a flight attendant two years ago.

    A Right   **B** Wrong   **C** Doesn't say

23 Ryan finds his work boring sometimes.

    A Right   **B** Wrong   **C** Doesn't say

24 Ryan feels afraid if he is flying in bad weather.

    A Right   **B** Wrong   **C** Doesn't say

25 Ryan says there is a night flight from London to Tenerife once a week.

    A Right   **B** Wrong   **C** Doesn't say

26 Ryan and his colleagues get free air tickets.

    A Right   **B** Wrong   **C** Doesn't say

27 Ryan spends all his holidays in Lanzarote.

    A Right   **B** Wrong   **C** Doesn't say

Reading and Writing • Part 5

What do I have to do?

- You need to choose the correct words to complete a short text.
- There are eight spaces in the text (28-35) and an example at the beginning (0).
- There are three options to fill each space (A, B or C).
- This part of the exam tests grammar. The words tested may be things like:
  (a) verb tenses and forms (*go, goes, went, gone*)
  (b) modal verbs (*might, should, can*)
  (c) auxiliary verbs (*be, have, do*)
  (d) pronouns (*she, her, us, ours*)
  (e) comparatives and superlatives (*bigger, the biggest, more exciting, the best*)
  (f) conjunctions (*and, or, but*)

How do I do it?

- Read the instructions so you know what the text will be about. There might be a picture to help you too.
- Read the whole article so you can understand the basic meaning.
- Look at the words that come before and after each space.
- Try all the options in the space before making your choice.
- For some questions, you might need to read the sentences before the one you are looking at. For example, if you are choosing between *he, she* or *they*.

Exam Extra!

Five key grammar rules

Correct the example sentences for each rule:

1 Remember to match the verb to the subject.

   ✗ *My sister like strawberry ice cream.*

   ✓ _____

2 Remember to use the correct verb tense (past, present or future).

   ✗ *I watch a great film last night.*

   ✓ _____

3 Remember to use *be* at the start of yes/no questions.

   ✗ *Today is your birthday?*

   ✓ _____

4 Remember to use *do* or *did* to make questions with other verbs.

   ✗ *Your teacher wears a tie every day?*

   ✓ _____

5 Remember to use *s* to make plural nouns.

   ✗ *My brother has got 200 CD!*

   ✓ _____

Over to you

Questions 28–35

Read the article about Central Park in New York.
Choose the best word (**A, B** or **C**) for each space.
For questions **28–35**, mark **A, B** or **C** on your answer sheet.

Central Park

Central Park is not the **(0)** _____ park in New York City, but it is the most famous. It has **(28)** _____ in many films and TV programmes, **(29)** _____ it is known by people all over the world.

Central Park is 150 years old, and more than 20 million people **(30)** _____ it each year. It has a large lake and many tall and beautiful trees. Some people think it is **(31)** _____ of the best places in the country to watch birds. **(32)** _____ are more than 230 different kinds here.

The park is also very popular with people **(33)** _____ like sport. Park Drive is a 10 kilometre road around the park and is used **(34)** _____ running, cycling and skating. In the summer months you **(35)** _____ see concerts, plays and film shows nearly every weekend.

Example:

| **0** | **A** big | **B** bigger | **C** biggest | *Answer:* | **0** | A ☐ B ☐ C ■ |

28	**A** be	**B** was	**C** been
29	**A** so	**B** but	**C** if
30	**A** visits	**B** visiting	**C** visit
31	**A** few	**B** one	**C** some
32	**A** There	**B** They	**C** Here
33	**A** where	**B** which	**C** who
34	**A** as	**B** for	**C** by
35	**A** must	**B** should	**C** can

Reading and Writing • Part 6

What do I have to do?

- You need to read some descriptions and write the correct words.
- There are descriptions of five words (36-40) and an example (0).
- The first letter of each word is there to help you.
- There are spaces to tell you how many letters are in each word.
- You must spell the words correctly.

How do I do it?

- Look at the instructions to find the topic for the words.
- Read the descriptions carefully. Look out for words like *these* which tell you that you need a plural word.
- Count the number of spaces to see how many letters you need. If you have too many letters or not enough letters, you have chosen the wrong word or spelled it incorrectly.
- Check your spelling carefully. You must spell the words correctly in this part of the exam.
- Write your answers clearly so the examiner can read them.

Over to you

Question 36–40

Read the descriptions **(36–40)** of some things you might find in the bedroom.
What is the word for each one?
The first letter is already there. There is one space for each other letter in the word.
For questions **36–40**, write the words on your answer sheet.

Example:

0   This tells you when to get up in the morning.   c _ _ _ _

0	clock

---

36   You put your head on this when you go to sleep.   p _ _ _ _ _

37   If you have a lot of books you will need these on the wall.   s _ _ _ _ _ _

38   You use this for playing games and doing your homework.   c _ _ _ _ _ _ _

39   You look at this when you comb your hair.   m _ _ _ _ _

40   If you want to read in bed you need this.   l _ _ _

Reading and Writing • Part 7

What do I have to do?

- You need to write words in the spaces to complete a short text, like an email, note or postcard.
- Sometimes there are two shorter texts, for example two emails.
- There are ten spaces to fill (41–50), and an example at the beginning (0).
- You need to write one word in each space.
- This part of the exam tests your knowledge of grammar.

How do I do it?

- Read the text (or texts) before you begin so that you know what it is about.
- Look at the words before and after each gap, and think about what kind of word you need. For example, you might need an article (*the*, *a*), a pronoun (*he*, *him*, *his*), or a preposition (*to*, *by*, *for*).
- Look at the other sentences near the gap. Think about the time being talked about (past, present or future).
- Remember, you must only write one word in each space, or you will not get the mark.
- Read through the text (or texts) when you have finished to check your answers
- Your spelling must be perfect, so check it carefully.

Over to you

Questions 41–50

Complete this postcard.
Write ONE word for each space.
For questions **41–50**, write the words on your answer sheet.

Example: | **0** | having |

Dear Monika,

I'm **(0)** _____ a great holiday in Spain. There's so **(41)** _____ to do on our campsite. There is a games room, a pool, and a place **(42)** _____ play tennis and football. And it's close to the sea **(43)** _____ we can go swimming every day.

There is a famous castle about 5km **(44)** _____ here, which is 1000 years **(45)** _____. Mum and Dad want to go and see **(46)** _____ tomorrow. Then **(47)** _____ Tuesday, we plan to rent bicycles and go for **(48)** _____ ride in the countryside.

I'll call you **(49)** _____ I get back and you can tell **(50)** _____ all about your holiday!

Love,
Sonia

Reading and Writing • Part 8

What do I have to do?

- You need to read two short texts and then complete some notes with information from the texts.
- The short texts will be things like advertisements, emails and notes.
- There are five pieces of information you need to find (51–55), and an example (0).
- The information you need might be days, dates, prices, times, names, or addresses.
- You might need to write one or two words.

How do I do it?

- Read the instructions and the two short texts so you understand the situation.
- Look at the notes and think about the information that you need to find. For example, you might need a time, a price or a place name.
- Read the texts carefully to find the right answer. There may be two pieces of information in the texts, but you must choose one answer. You will get no mark if you write two answers.
- You only need to give short answers, not full sentences. The answers will be a number, or one or two words.
- You must spell all words correctly, so copy them carefully and use capital letters where necessary.
- Write numbers (1, 2, 3), not words (one, two, three), so you don't make any spelling mistakes.

Exam Extra!

Reading carefully

There will usually be two possible answers to each question, so you have to read carefully to see which one is right.

Read the sentence and then answer the question.

1 I've already seen *Dark Mountain* so let's go and see *Holiday Time* instead.

   Which film will they see?

2 Tickets cost £10 last year, but they're £5 more this year. Do you think people will be happy to pay £15?

   How much are the tickets this year?

3 I'd love to go shopping this weekend! Are you free on Saturday? I'm afraid I'm busy all day Sunday.

   What day does she want to go shopping?

4 The courses begin on 9th or 16th February. I prefer the earlier date.

   When does he want to start the course?

5 Hi, Pete, I'll bring drinks for both of us tomorrow. But don't forget your camera, mine's broken!

   What should Pete bring tomorrow?

Over to you

Questions 51–55

Read the email and the ticket about a school party.
Complete Suzy's notes.
For questions **51–55**, write the information on the answer sheet.

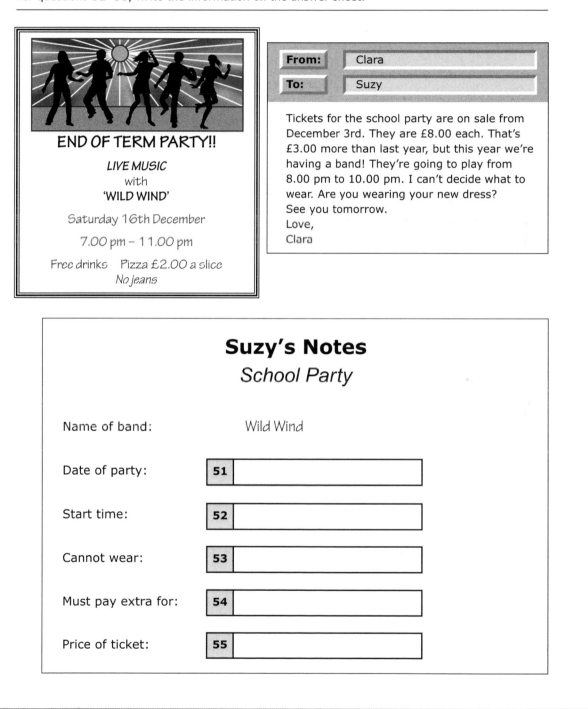

END OF TERM PARTY!!

LIVE MUSIC
with
'WILD WIND'

Saturday 16th December

7.00 pm – 11.00 pm

Free drinks   Pizza £2.00 a slice
No jeans

| From: | Clara |
| To: | Suzy |

Tickets for the school party are on sale from December 3rd. They are £8.00 each. That's £3.00 more than last year, but this year we're having a band! They're going to play from 8.00 pm to 10.00 pm. I can't decide what to wear. Are you wearing your new dress?
See you tomorrow.
Love,
Clara

Suzy's Notes
School Party

Name of band:	Wild Wind
Date of party:	**51**
Start time:	**52**
Cannot wear:	**53**
Must pay extra for:	**54**
Price of ticket:	**55**

Reading and Writing • Part 9

What do I have to do?

- You need to write an email, postcard or note to a friend.
- There are three things that you have to tell your friend.
- The question might include a message from your friend asking for three pieces of information, or it might tell you the three points that you must write about.
- You should write between 25 and 35 words.

How do I do it?

- Read the instrcutions carefully to understand the situation.
- Start your letter with *Hi*, *Hello* or *Dear* and the name of the person you are writing to.
- Find the three things you need to write about and make sure you write about them. You will lose marks if you only write about one or two points.
- Make sure you write about the correct time (past, present or future).
- Finish your letter with *from* and your name.
- Read your lettter carefully to check for mistakes. You should spell words correctly, write proper sentences, and use CAPITAL letters and punctuation correctly.
- Check you have written the right amount of words. If you write less than 25 words, you will lose marks. If you write more than 35 words, you might make more mistakes.

What does it look like?

Question 56

Read this email from your English friend, Charlie.

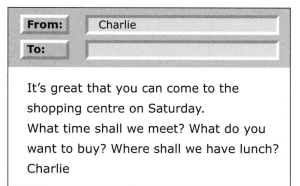

From:	Charlie
To:	

It's great that you can come to the shopping centre on Saturday.
What time shall we meet? What do you want to buy? Where shall we have lunch?
Charlie

Write an email to Charlie and answer the questions.
Write **25–35** words.
Write the email on your answer sheet.

How does it work?

1 Read these example answers to Part 9 and answer the questions below.

1 Which one answers all three points?
2 Which one answers only two points?
3 Which one has mistakes with punctuation?
4 Which one is too short?
5 Which one has forgotten something?

A

I like to eat in the Pizza Express at lunchtime in the shopping centre.

I would buy some CDs.

See you

Ahmed

B

I'll go to the Lakeside shopping Centre at 9.30 in the morning.

I hope you are there. I must buy a T shirt and some jeans.

I like to have a lunch in Macdonalds, how about you?

Juan

C

ok we meet in the shopping centre at 13 o'clock we have sandwiches for

lunch in the park and i will buy one football magazine and some chocolate.

2 Correct the mistakes in the example answers.

Listening • Part 1

What do I have to do?

- You will hear five short dialogues and one example.
- There is a question for each dialogue (1–5) and three possible answers (A, B or C).
- The answers can be pictures, words or numbers.
- You need to listen and choose the correct answer.

How do I do it?

- There will be a short pause before each question, so read the question to find out what information you are listening for. You will also hear the question.
- Look at the pictures and think about the words you might hear.
- All three pictures will be talked about, so you need to listen to the whole conversation before you choose your answer.
- Listen to the whole dialogue before choosing your answer because the correct answer might be at the beginning, in the middle, or at the end of the dialogue.
- You will hear the conversation twice, so don't worry if you don't get the answer at first.

What do I hear?

Here is the transcript for Question 1:

PHILLIP:	Have you done your history project, Lizzie? Don't we have to give it to the teacher on Monday? I haven't started mine yet!
LIZZIE:	Don't worry, we've got more time than that. She doesn't want it until Friday now.
PHILLIP:	Really? When did she tell us that?
LIZZIE:	In the lesson on Wednesday. Weren't you listening, Phillip?

🔊 26 *Over to you*

Questions 1–5

You will hear five short conversations.
You will hear each conversation twice.
There is one question for each conversation.
For each question, choose the right answer (**A**, **B** or **C**).

Example: How many people were at the party?

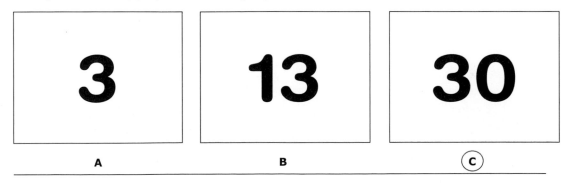

3	**13**	**30**
A	**B**	Ⓒ

1   When must they give the homework to the teacher?

Monday	Wednesday	Friday
A	**B**	**C**

2   What will Melissa and her Mum buy?

   A   **B**   **C**

3   What time does the basketball match begin?

   A   **B**   **C**

4   Which is Sandra's house?

 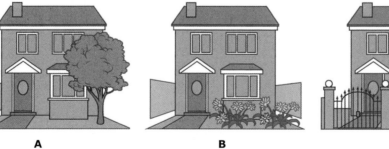

   A   **B**   **C**

5   Which computer game will the boys play now?

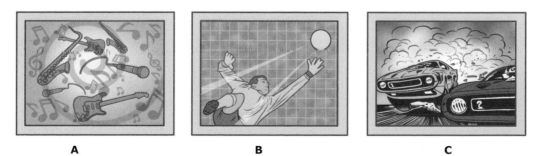

   A   **B**   **C**

Listening • Part 2

What do I have to do?

- You will hear a conversation between two people who know each other.
- You need to match the things in the two lists.
- The list on the left (questions 6-10) could be things like people's names, days of the week, or times.
- The list on the right (answers A-H) could be words on one topic, for example food, school subjects or colours, or they could be adjectives giving people's opinions.
- There are five questions and an example (0), but there are eight answers. So there are two answers that you do not need to use.

How do I do it?

- Before you listen, look at the instructions to see what the conversation is about.
- Look at the two lists and think about the words you might hear.
- You will hear the information about questions 6-10 talked about in the same order as on your question paper.
- You might hear all the words (A-H), but they will not all be the correct answers.
- Think about the meaning of the words in A-H. Sometimes the words you hear will be different. For example, you may read *sport* and hear *football* and *tennis*.
- If you cannot answer a question, go on to the next question. You will hear the conversation twice, so you can try again.
- If you cannot answer a question after listening twice, write one of the answers you haven't used – it may be the right answer!

What do I hear?

Here is part of the transcript:

TIM:	Hi, Mia. How was school?
MIA:	Hi, Tim. Good. We did a class project to find out people's favourite TV programmes. There were some surprises.
TIM:	I know what you like best – cartoons!
MIA:	That's right. And everyone knows Rob loves anything to do with plants and animals.
TIM:	Your friend Hannah's a great cook, she must watch all the cooking shows.
MIA:	You're wrong. She's a big fan of rock and reggae so she loves any concerts on TV.

Question 6–10

Listen to Mia and Tim talking about favourite television programmes.
What programme does each person like best?
For questions **6–10**, write a letter **(A–H)** next to each person.
You will hear the conversation twice.

Example:

0 Mia | A |

	PEOPLE			PROGRAMMES
6	Rob		**A**	cartoons
7	Hannah		**B**	cooking
			C	film
8	Carl		**D**	music
9	Rosie		**E**	nature
			F	quiz
10	Tim		**G**	sport
			H	travel

Listening • Part 3

What do I have to do?

- You will hear a conversation between two people.
- There are five questions (11–15) and an example (0).
- There are three possible answers to each question (A, B or C).
- The answers can be words or numbers.
- You need to listen and choose the correct answer to each question.

How do I do it?

- There is some time before you listen, so read the instructions and questions to find out what the conversation is about.
- You will hear the information you need in the same order as the questions.
- You will hear something about all three options for each question. Listen carefully to find the correct answer.
- If you cannot answer a question, go on to the next question. You will hear the conversation twice, so you can try again.

What do I hear?

Here is part of the transcript:

FELICITY:	Hi, Daniel. I missed yesterday's meeting about the school camping trip. Are we still going on the 15th of May?
DANIEL:	We leave on the 29th now, Felicity. But we have to pay by the 22nd.
FELICITY:	OK. How much is it?
DANIEL:	It's £55 for the campsite and £27 for the food, so it's £82 all together.
FELICITY:	That's not bad. What do we have to bring?
DANIEL:	Well, the campsite has tents for us, but we need our own sleeping bags. We can use the school's plates and cups.

Questions 11–15

Listen to Felicity asking Daniel about a school trip.
For each question choose the right answer **A**, **B** or **C**.
You will hear the conversation twice.

Example:

0   The school trip will begin on

    A   15th May.

    B   22nd May.

    (C)   29th May.

---

11   How much does the trip cost?

    A   £27

    B   £55

    C   £82

12   What must everyone bring?

    A   a sleeping bag

    B   a plate and cup

    C   a tent

13   The campsite is

    A   in the mountains.

    B   on a farm.

    C   on the beach.

14   This year they will not

    A   go walking.

    B   go climbing.

    C   go swimming.

15   What time will the coach leave?

    A   6.00 a.m.

    B   6.15 a.m.

    C   6.30 a.m.

Listening • **Part 4** and **Part 5**

What do I have to do?

- In Part 4, you will hear a conversation between two people.
- In Part 5, you will hear some information from one speaker.
- You need to listen and complete the notes.
- There are five spaces to fill (16-20 in Part 4, 21-25 in Part 5) in the notes and an example.
- You might need to listen for a number or a spelling.
- Some of the answers are one word and some are two words.

How do I do it?

- Before you listen, look at the instructions so you know what the conversation or information is about.
- Look at the form and think about the information you will be listening for. For example, you might need to listen for a day, a time, a price, a place or a telephone number.
- You might hear two possible answers (two times or two prices). Listen carefully to choose the right one.
- You should try to spell words correctly. If a word is spelled out, you must spell it correctly.
- Write numbers as numbers (25) not words (twenty-five), so you don't make a mistake with the spelling.
- You will hear the conversation twice, so use the second listening to check your answers. Try to write something in each space − even if you are not sure about the answer.
- Make notes while you listen. Then write your answers clearly on the answer sheet so the examiner can easily read them.

What do I hear?

Here is part of the transcript for Part 4:

Ros:	Why don't you come to the Art Club at the museum on Saturday, Dan?
Dan:	Oh I don't know…
Ros:	You won't have to get up early. It starts at ten thirty and it finishes at half past twelve. It's really good fun.
Dan:	But you know I'm no good at painting.
Ros:	That doesn't matter. Last week we made animals out of card and next time we're making posters to put on the wall.

Over to you

🔊 **29** *Part 4*

Questions 16–20

You will hear a conversation about an art club.
Listen and complete each question.
You will hear the conversation twice.

Museum Art Club

Day:	Saturday
Begins at:	(16) ....
Next week they will make:	(17) ....
One meeting costs:	(18) £ ....
Place:	(19) .... in the museum
Bring:	(20) ....

🔊 **30** *Part 5*

Questions 21–25

You will hear a boy leaving a message for a friend.
Listen and complete each question.
You will hear the information twice.

Trip to Cinema

With:	Graham
Address of cinema:	(21) ....
Price of ticket:	(22) £ ....
Time to meet Graham:	(23) .... p.m.
Meet Graham in the:	(24) .... next to the cinema
Graham's mobile number:	(25) ....

The Speaking Test

About the Speaking Test

- The Speaking Test takes between eight and ten minutes.
- You do the test with a partner.
- There are two examiners. One examiner asks you and your partner questions. The other examiner just listens.

Exam Extra!

Different ways of asking the same question

Match the questions with similar meanings.

1 How old are you?

2 Do you have any brothers and sisters?

3 What are your hobbies?

4 Do you have any pets?

5 What's your favourite subject at school?

6 What do your parents do?

A Do you have a big family?

B What do you like to do at the weekend?

C Do you like studying Science?

D When is your birthday?

E What are your mother and father's jobs?

F Have you got a dog?

Speaking • Part 1

What do I have to do?

- You need to answer the examiner's questions.
- The questions are about your life – your house, your school, your hobbies, your family, and things you like and dislike.
- You need to spell your surname for one of the questions.
- The examiner also asks your partner some questions.
- This part of the test takes about five minutes.

How do I do it?

- Listen carefully, because the examiner will not ask you the same questions as your partner.
- Speak clearly and ask the examiner to repeat the question if you don't understand.
- Try to give full answers, not just one word.

Speaking • Part 2

What do I have to do?

- You need to talk to your partner in this part of the test.
- The examiner will give each person a card. One card is some information (for example, an advertisement or an invitation). The other card has some words on it to make five questions from.
- The person with the question card asks their questions. The other person uses the information to answer the questions.
- Afterwards, the examiner will give you two different cards so you can swap roles and do the activity again.

How do I do it?

- Speak to your partner not the examiner.
- Use the prompts to help you make full questions.
- Listen to your partner's questions and give answers in full sentences. Don't just read the words from the card.
- If you don't understand your partner, say, 'Can you repeat that please?'
- Don't worry if you make a mistake. Try to enjoy the test!

Exam Extra!

What do I do if I don't understand?

If you don't understand a question, you can ask for help. Look at these phrases.

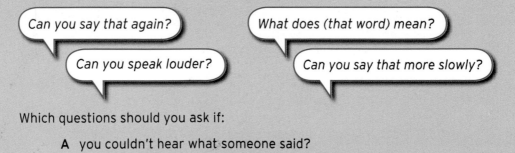

Which questions should you ask if:

  A you couldn't hear what someone said?

  B you do not understand a word?

  C someone is speaking too quickly?

How does it work?

> Candidate A, here is some information about an internet café.

> Candidate B, you don't know anything about the internet café, so ask A some questions about it.

> Now B, ask A your questions about the internet café and A, you answer them.

STARBYTES CAFÉ

22 Cross Street

Surf the internet,
play games,
send emails

£3 per hour
15 computers

Hot and cold drinks and snacks

Open 10 am — 7 pm

Internet café

- where?
- when / open?
- what / do there?
- sell / food?
- cost? £?

> Candidate B, here is some information about a new computer game.

> Candidate A, you don't know anything about the computer game so ask B some questions about it.

> Now A, ask B your questions about the computer game and A, you answer them.

An exciting new computer game for 1–4 players

ROAD HOGS

Choose your car and race around the city

£30 FROM ALL COMPUTER SHOPS
OR FROM WWW.GAMESCO.COM

NEW COMPUTER GAME

- NAME?
- PRICE? £?
- FUN?
- WHERE / BUY?
- HOW MANY PLAYERS?

Language summary

Unit 1

Introducing yourself

I'm	Luis.
I'm	from Spain.
I'm	Spanish.

We use *I'm* to give personal information.

- *Hi. I'm Sara. I'm from Canada.*

Introductions

We use *Nice to meet you* when we meet someone for the first time.

- *Hello, Sara. Nice to meet you.*

We use *This is...* to introduce someone.

- *This is my brother, James.*

Asking about someone else

How	old are you?
What's	your name?
What's	your address?
Where	are you from?

We use questions with *how*, *what* and *where* to ask about someone when we meet them.

- *Hi, I'm Tim. What's your name?*

The question *How are you?* asks about someone's health.

- *Hi. How are you?*
- *I'm fine, thanks.*

Spelling

We use capital letters at the start of names and countries.

- *James is from Canada.*
- *Yukiko is from Japan.*

We use *double* to give spellings.

- *Will is spelled W - I - double L.*
- *My surname is Moss. That's M - O - double S.*

Present simple

+		I / you / We / They	work.
		He / She / It	works.
–		I / You / We / They	don't work.
		He / She / It	doesn't work.
?	Do	I / you / we / they	work?
	Does	he / she / it	work?

We use the present simple to talk about things we do every day, and to talk about likes and dislikes.

- *I go to a theatre school.*
- *I don't have English every day.*
- *What do you have on Monday?*
- *She doesn't like singing.*

Remember that in positive sentences, we add *-s* or *-es* in *he*, *she* and *it* forms.

- *He plays football every day.*
- *She goes to a theatre school.*
- *She studies singing.*

Adverbs of frequency

100%	→	→	→	0%
always	usually	often	sometimes	never

We use frequency adverbs to say how often we do something.

- *He always plays football in the afternoon.*
- *I never enjoy Maths.*

In negative sentences, adverbs of frequency come between *don't* or *doesn't* and the verb.

- *I don't always have Geography on monday.*
- *He doesn't usually play matches in the morning.*

Unit 2

Making questions

Question word		
Who	is	that boy?
When	is	your birthday?
Where	do	you live?
What	does	she look like?
Which boy	is	your brother?
What pets	have	you got?
How many sisters	have	you got?

We can make questions with *who, when, where,* and *what*. *Be, do,* and *have* come before the subject.

- *When is your birthday?*
- *What does she look like?*
- *How many pets have you got?*

Have got

+		I / you / We / They	have got...
		He / She	has got...
–		I / You / We / They	haven't got...
		He / She	hasn't got...
?	Have	I / you / we / they	got...?
	Has	he / she / it	got...?

We can use *have got* or *have* with the same meaning.

- *He has two sisters.*
- *He's got two sisters.*

Notice how we form negative sentences and questions.

- *He doesn't have any brothers.*
- *He hasn't got any brothers.*

- *Do you have blue eyes?*
- *Have you got blue eyes?*

Describing people

We use *be* with adjectives.

- *She is pretty.*
- *He is quite old.*

We use *have* or *have got* with nouns.

- *He's got long hair.*
- *She's got big blue eyes.*

Present continuous

+	I	am	working.
	He / She / It	is	working.
	You / We / They	are	working.
–	I	'm not	working.
	He / She / It	isn't	working.
	You / We / They	aren't	working.
?	Am	I	working?
	Is	he / she / it	working?
	Are	you / we / they	working?

We use the present continuous to talk about something we are doing now.

- *I can't come to the door. I'm washing my hair at the moment.*
- *Paul is busy at the moment. He's doing his homework.*
- *Where is Sara? Is she watching TV?*

Present tenses

Compare the present simple and the present continuous.

- *Jack plays football every Saturday.*
  (= He often does this.)
- *Jack is playing football at the moment.*
  (= He is doing this now.)

Look at the difference between these questions.

- *What does he do? (= What is his job?)*
- *What is he doing? (= at the moment)*

Unit 3

Talking about activities

We use *play* for team sports.

- *Shall we play football?*
- *He's playing baseball.*
- *We play tennis on Wednesdays.*

We use *go* for activities you can do alone.

- *Let's go swimming.*
- *I go shopping on Saturdays.*
- *She often goes running.*

We use *go to* for places.

- *Let's go to the cinema.*
- *What time shall we go to the park?*
- *We go to school by bus.*

Making suggestions

We can use *let's*, *shall we*, *how about* and *what about* to make suggestions for activities.

- *Let's do something!*
- *How about going somewhere today?*

We use *let's...* and *shall we...* with the infinitive.

- *Let's watch a film tonight.*
- *Shall we play a computer game?*

We use *how about...* and *what about...* with the *-ing* form.

- *How about watching a football match?*
- *What about going to a restaurant?*

We can also use *shall we...* in *wh-* questions.

- *What time shall we meet?*
- *What shall we watch?*

Accepting and rejecting suggestions

We can use special phrases to accept a suggestion.

- *That's a great idea.*
- *That sounds great.*

We often give a reason why we don't want to do something.

- *No, I don't like baseball.*
- *Sorry, I can't. I have to study.*

Making requests

		Verb	Object
Can	*you*	*bring*	*some drinks?*
Could	*you*	*open*	*the door?*

We can use *Can you...* and *Could you...* to ask for help.

- *Can you help me?*
- *Could you open the door for me?*

Making offers

		Verb	Object
Can	*I*	*make*	*some cake?*
Shall	*I*	*open*	*the window?*

We can use *Can I...* and *Shall I...* to offer to help someone.

- *Can I help you?*
- *Shall I open the door for you?*

Imperatives

We use imperatives to tell someone to do something.

- *Open the door.*
- *Give me that book.*

We use *don't* + imperatives to tell someone not to do something.

- *Don't open the door.*
- *Don't eat that cake.*

We don't use a subject in imperative sentences.

- *Shut the door.* (NOT *You shut the door.*)

We usually use imperatives with close friends or family. We use *please*, *can you...* or *could you...* to be more polite.

- *Can you shut the door please?*
- *Please don't eat that cake.*

Unit 4

Past simple

+		I	went	shopping.
		They	bought	some clothes.
–		I	didn't go	shopping.
		They	didn't buy	any clothes.
?	Did	you	go	shopping?
	Did	they	buy	any clothes?

We use the past simple for things that happened in the past.

- *I went shopping yesterday.*
- *She met her friends last night.*

For regular verbs, we form the past simple with *-ed*.

- *We looked at some clothes.*
- *She listened to some music.*

Some verbs are irregular.

- *He bought a magazine.*
- *She ate some chocolate.*

We use *did / didn't* + verb to form negatives and questions.

- *She didn't buy anything.*
- *Where did they go?*

Past simple of *to be*

+	I / He / She / It	was...
	You / We / They	were...
–	I / He / She / It	wasn't...
	You / We / They	weren't...
?	Was	I / he / she / it ...?
	Were	you / we / they ...?

The simple past forms of *be* are *was* and *were*.

- *The phone was expensive.*
- *The shops were closed.*

Relative pronouns

Relative pronoun	Gives more information about...
who	a person
which	a thing
where	a place

We use relative pronouns to add more information to a sentence.

We use *who* to add information about a person.

- *My sister, who is twelve, loves horses.*
- *This is my friend Sara, who lives on a boat.*

We use *which* to add information about a thing.

- *I've got a computer, which I use for doing my homework.*
- *This photo, which my sister took, is of our holiday in France.*

We use *where* to add information about a place.

- *This is my bedroom, where I sleep.*
- *This is the park where we play football.*

This, that, these and *those*

Singular	Plural
This is my bedroom.	**These are my books.**
That's my desk.	**Those are my CDs.**

We use *this* and *these* to talk about things that are near to us.

- *This is my guitar.*
- *These are my shoes.*

We use *that* and *those* to talk about things that are further away from us.

- *That's my desk, over there.*
- *Those are my CDs, on the shelf by the window.*

Unit 5

Countable and uncountable nouns

Countable nouns	Uncountable nouns
carrot, carrots potato, potatoes lemon, lemons	milk cheese butter

Countable nouns have a singular and a plural form. Uncountable nouns don't have a plural form.

- one carrot, two potatoes
- some milk (NOT one milk, two milks)

Some, any, how much, how many

Plural countable nouns	Uncountable nouns
There are some carrots.	There is some cheese.
There aren't any carrots.	There isn't any cheese.
How many carrots?	How much cheese?

We use some and any with plural countable nouns and uncountable nouns.

We use some in affirmative sentences, and in offers.

- We've got some potatoes.
- Would you like some cheese?

We use any in negative sentences and factual questions.

- We haven't got any milk.
- Have we got any carrots?

We use how much and how many to ask about quantity. We use how much with uncountable nouns, and how many with plural countable nouns.

- How much milk do we need?
- How many grapes have you got?

Plural nouns

Most nouns	add -s	carrot → carrots grape → grapes
nouns ending in -ch, -o, -s, -sh and -x	add -es	potato → potatoes box → boxes
nouns ending in -f or -fe	take off -f or -fe and add -ves	knife → knives

Containers

We use containers with of + the food or drink.

- Can I have a box of cereal?
- Let's buy three cans of soup.

We can use containers to talk about quantity for uncountable things.

- We need three bottles of water.
- There are three bags of sugar in the cupboard.

Ordering food

	Verb		
I'd	like	a salad.	
I'll	have	a burger.	
Can I	have	some chips?	
–	–	Some pizza	for me, please.

We can use these expressions to order food.

- I'd like some chocolate.
- Some chips for me, please.

Offering food

		Verb	
Would	you	like	a dessert?
Do	you	want	some water?
What	about	–	a chocolate brownie?

We can use these expressions to offer food to someone.

- Would you like some chips?
- What about some ice cream?

Note: We use Do you like...? to ask for someone's opinion, but we use Would you like...? to offer something to someone.

- 'Do you like chicken?' 'Yes, I do. I love chicken!'
- 'Would you like some chips?' 'Yes, please. I'm really hungry!'

Unit 6

Pronouns

Subject	Object	Possessive + object	Possessive + no object
I	me	my	mine
you	you	your	yours
he	him	his	his
she	her	her	hers
it	it	its	its
we	us	our	ours
they	the	their	theirs

We use subject pronouns as the subject of a verb.

• *I like comedies.*
• *He wants to go to the cinema.*

We use object pronouns as the object of a verb.

• *The film made me cry.*
• *She ate them all.*

We use possessive pronouns to show possession.

• *These are my sweets.*
• *Those sweets are yours.*

Possessive 's and s'

We use 's and s' to show possession. We use 's for one person and s' for more than one person.

• *She ate her friend's popcorn.*
  (= just one friend)
• *She ate her friends' popcorn.*
  (= more than one friend)

But we use 's with children.

• *Where are the children's tickets?*

Modals for ability

Affirmative	Negative
can	can't
could	couldn't

We use *can* and *can't* to talk about ability in the present.

• *He can play the guitar.*
• *She can't sing.*

We use *could* and *couldn't* to talk about ability in the past.

• *He could play the piano when he was three.*
• *She couldn't go to the festival last summer.*

Modals for obligation

Obligation	No obligation	Not allowed
must	–	mustn't
have to	don't have to	–
need to	needn't	–
had to	–	–

We use *must*, *have to* and *need to* for obligation in the present.

• *You must pay for your tickets.*
• *We have to arrive at 9 o'clock.*
• *You need to bring a coat.*

Notice the difference between *don't have to / needn't* and *mustn't*.

• *You don't have to / needn't leave now.*
  (= there is no obligation)
• *You mustn't leave now.*
  (= it's not allowed)

We use *had to* to talk about obligation in the past.

• *I had to play the piano when I was a child.*

Unit 7

Conjunctions

Sara likes wearing dresses	but	I always wear jeans.
I wear a coat	when	it is cold.
I often wear these jeans	because	I like them.

We use conjunctions to join two sentences together.

We use *and* when the sentences are similar, and we use *but* when they are different.

- Sara likes skirts and she likes dresses.
- Sara likes skirts but Gemma likes jeans.

We use *or* to give an alternative.

- I usually wear a jacket, or I sometimes wear a coat.

We use *because* to give a reason, and we use *so* to give a result.

- He was cold because he was wearing shorts and a T-shirt.
- He was cold so he put on a sweater.

We use *when* and *if* to talk about a time or a particular situation.

- I wear a coat when it's cold.
- He usually wears shorts if it's hot.

A pair of

	pair	of	Plural noun
a	pair	of	shoes
a	pair	of	trousers

We use *a pair of* when there are two things.

- a pair of trainers
- a pair of boots

We also use *a pair of* for things with two parts.

- a pair of sunglasses
- a pair of trousers

Verbs with *-ing* or *to* + infinitive

Verb with infinitive + *to*	Verb with *-ing*	Verbs with *-ing* or *to* + infinitive
want	like	start
would like	love	begin
hope	hate	continue
decide	enjoy	stop
promise	finish	try
learn		

Some verbs are followed by *to* + infinitive, and some are followed by *-ing*.

- I want to go to the festival.
- I like going to festivals.

With some verbs, both are possible.
- She started dancing.
- She started to dance.

Some verbs can use both, but have different meanings.

- I stopped studying.
  (= I was studying, but then I stopped and did something else.)

- I stopped to study.
  (= I stopped doing something because I wanted to study.)

- I remember going to the festival.
  (= I went and I remember it.)

- I remembered to go to the festival.
  (= I did not forget to go.)

Notice the difference between *like* and *would like.*

- She likes planning the costumes.
  (= she enjoys it)
- She would like to plan the costumes.
  (= she wants to)

Unit 8

Asking how people feel

We can use different questions to ask about someone's health if we think they are sick.

- *What's wrong?*
- *What's the matter?*
- *Are you OK?*

Talking about how you feel

I've	*got*	*a headache.*
I	*feel*	*sick.*
I don't	*feel*	*well.*

We can use *I've got*, *I feel* and *I don't feel* to talk about how we feel.

- *I've got the flu.*
- *I've got a headache.*
- *I feel sleepy.*
- *I don't feel very well.*

We can also use *my ... hurts.*

- *My stomach hurts!*

Advice

		Verb	
You	*should*	*take*	*this medicine.*
You	*shouldn't*	*go*	*to bed late.*

We can use *you should* and *you shouldn't* to give advice.
- *You should be careful.*
- *You shouldn't eat too much chocolate.*

We can also use *Why don't you...?* to give advice.

- *Why don't you go to the doctor?*

Possibility

		Verb	
She	*might*	*have*	*a temperature.*
Your leg	*may*	*be*	*broken.*
We	*might not*	*visit*	*you tomorrow.*
Your arm	*may not*	*be*	*broken.*

We can use *may* and *might* to talk about things that are possible but not certain.

- *She might have the flu.*
- *He may be ill.*
- *They might not let me go home today.*

First conditional

If clause	main clause
If you go out in the rain,	*you will get wet.*
If you don't play well,	*you won't win.*

main clause	if clause
You will get wet	*if you go out in the rain.*
You won't win	*if you don't play well.*

We use the first conditional to talk about things that are likely to happen.

We use the present simple in the *if* clause, and we use *will / won't* in the main clause.

- *If you win the race, you will get a prize.*
  (NOT *If you will win the race...*)
- *If you don't do any sport, you won't be very healthy.*

Will is often shortened to 'll.

- *If you eat a lot of chocolate, you'll get fat.*

We can put the *if* clause or the main clause first in the sentence. When the *if* clause is first, we use a comma.

- *You'll enjoy this sport if you try it.*
- *If you try this sport, you'll enjoy it.*

Unit 9

Comparatives and superlatives

Adjective	Comparative	Superlative
small	smaller	the smallest
big	bigger	the biggest
pretty	prettier	the prettiest
dangerous	more dangerous	the most dangerous

We use comparatives to compare two things.

• *Mice are smaller than cats.*

We use superlatives to compare three or more things.

• *What is the biggest animal?*
  (= bigger than all the others)

For short adjectives, we add -*er* and -*est*.

• *fast* ➜ *faster* ➜ *the fastest*

For adjectives ending in y, we add -*ier* and -*iest*.

• *friendly* ➜ *friendlier* ➜ *friendliest*

For adjectives ending in a vowel + consonant, we double the final consonant.

• *big* ➜ *bigger* ➜ *biggest*

For long adjectives, we use *more* and *the most*.

• *beautiful* ➜ *more beautiful* ➜ *the most beautiful*

Notice that we use *than* after comparative adjectives.

• *Monkeys are more intelligent than horses.*

Irregular adjectives

Adjective	Comparative	Superlative
good	better	the best
bad	worse	the worst

Some adjectives are irregular.

• *Dolphins are better swimmers than cats.*
• *Snakes are the worst pets!*

Going to and *will*

Subject	be	going to	verb
I	am	going to	cycle to school.
You / We / They	are	going to	be late.
It	is	going to	rain.

Subject	will	verb
I	will	go to university.
You / We / They	will	go to the beach.
It	will	be cloudy tomorrow.

We use *going to* for plans, or for future actions we are sure about.

• *I'm going to go on holiday soon.*
• *Look at the sky! It's going to rain.*

We use *will* to guess about the future.

• *I think I'll be a teacher one day.*
• *What will the weather be like in 20 years?*

We often use words like *maybe, probably, perhaps* and *I think* with *will*.

• *Maybe it will be sunny tomorrow.*
• *It will probably snow in the winter.*
• *I think we'll go to the beach tomorrow.*

Talking about the weather

We can use verbs to talk about the weather.

• *It's raining.*
• *It's going to snow tomorrow.*

We can use adjectives to talk about the weather.

• *It's very cold today.*
• *It's windy.*

We can use nouns to talk about the weather.

• *There's a lot of snow today.*
• *Look at all that rain!*

Unit 10

Present continuous for future arrangements

We can use the present continuous to talk about future actions. We use the present continuous when we have a definite plan to do something.

- I'm meeting her friends at 10 o'clock tomorrow.
- We're going shopping on Saturday.
- He isn't going on holiday this summer.
- What are you doing at the weekend?

We cannot use the present simple with this meaning.

- I'm going to a concert tomorrow.
  (NOT I go to a concert tomorrow.)

Talking about transport

We use *catch* and *miss* for trains, buses and planes.

- We can catch the bus into town.
- Hurry up or we'll miss the train!

We use *get on* and *get off* for trains, buses and planes.

- When the bus stops, we can get on.
- It was lovely and sunny when we got off the plane.

We use *get in* and *get out of* for taxis and helicopters.

- We all got into the taxi.
- The helicopter landed and we got out.

We can use *catch* and *take* with most kinds of transport.

- Let's take a taxi to the airport.
- We caught a bus to the hotel.

We use *ride* with bicycles and motorbikes.

- My uncle rides a motorbike.
- I rode my bicycle to the lake.
  (= I cycled to the lake.)

Too and not enough

Subject	Verb		Adjective	
It	*is*	*too*	*cold.*	*–*
It	*isn't*	*–*	*warm*	*enough.*

We use *too* + adjective when there is more of something than we want.

- The buses are too crowded.
- The tickets are too expensive.

We use *not* + adjective + *enough* when we need more of something.

- This taxi isn't big enough for all of us!

We can also use *not enough* with nouns when we need more of something.

- I haven't got enough money!
- There aren't enough hotels.

Too and very

We use *very* to give an opinion of something.

- This coffee is very hot.
- The train to New York is very expensive.

We use *too* if we can't do something.

- This coffee is too hot.
  (= I can't drink it.)

- The train to New York is too expensive.
  (= I can't buy a ticket.)

Too much and too many

		too much / too many	Noun
There	**is**	too much	traffic.
There	**are**	too many	cars.

We use *too much* and *too many* with nouns, when there is more of something than we need. We use *too much* + uncountable nouns, and *too many* + plural countable nouns.

- It costs too much money!
- There are too many people on the bus!

Unit 11

Present perfect

+		I / You / We / They	have visited Paris.
		He / She / It	has visited Paris.
–		I / You / We / They	haven't visited Paris.
		He / She / It	hasn't visited Paris.
?	Have	I / you / we / they	visited Paris?
	Has	he / she / it	visited Paris?

We use the present perfect for things that happened sometime in the past.

- *She's been to Italy.*
- *They haven't seen that building.*
- *Have you tried the new restaurant?*

We use the simple past for things that happened at a definite time in the past.

- *She went to Italy last year.*
- *They didn't see that building yesterday.*
- *Did you try that new restaurant last night?*

For and *since*

for + amount of time	since + specific time
for two weeks for six months for an hour	since yesterday since last week since last year

We use the present perfect with *for* or *since* for actions that started in the past and continue in the present.

- *He has been here for two weeks.*
  (= He arrived two weeks ago, and he is still here.)
- *She has been in America since Friday.*
  (= She arrived on Friday and she is still there.)

Just, yet and *already*

We often use the present perfect with *just, yet* and *already*.

- *We've just finished.*
  (= We finished a short time ago.)
- *They haven't left yet.*
  (= They haven't left, but we expect they will soon.)
- *He has already arrived.*
  (= He arrived earlier than we expected.)

Giving directions

Verb		
Turn	left	at the traffic lights.
Turn	right	at the roundabout.
Take	the first road	on the left.
Go	past	the bank.
Go	straight on	at the crossroads.
Go	over	the bridge.

We use *How do I get to...* to ask for directions.

- *Excuse me, how do I get to the library?*

We use these expressions to give directions.

- *Go straight on, then turn left by the bank.*
- *Turn left at the crossroads, then go over the bridge.*

We can use *behind, between, in front of, next to* and *opposite* to say where something is.

- *The hotel is behind the swimming pool.*
- *The school is between the bank and the post office.*
- *My house is opposite the library.*
  (= on the other side of the road)

We can check we understand by repeating what the other person said.

- *Turn left at the bank. OK I've got it.*
- *So I go straight on and take the second right?*

We can use *take* to give the time needed to get somewhere.

- *It takes about five minutes on foot.*
- *It takes about 20 minutes by train.*

We can use *for* with distances.

- *Go straight on for about 500 metres.*

Unit 12

Believe, hope, know, say and *think*

	Verb	*that*	Object
I	think	*that*	technology is very useful.
I	hope	*that*	my computer works.
She	believes	*that*	I spend too much time online.
He	says	*that*	I watch too much TV.
I	know	*that*	I send a lot of text messages.

We use *believe, hope, know, say* and *think* to give opinions. We usually use *that* after these verbs.

• *My mum thinks that I spend too much time on my computer.*
• *I believe that the internet is very useful.*

To give negative opinions, we usually use *not + think*, but we use *hope + not*.

• *I don't think that I spend too much time chatting to my friends online.*
  (= I think that I don't spend too much time chatting.)
• *I hope that he doesn't spend all his time playing computer games!*

We can omit *that*.

• *I know (that) I spend a lot of time playing computer games.*

Talking about technology

We often use short versions of words to talk about technology.

• *I bought a new mobile yesterday.*
  (= I bought a new mobile phone yesterday.)
• *Have you got a PC?*
  (= Have you got a computer?)
• *I love surfing the net.*
  (= I love surfing the internet.)

Past continuous

+	I / He / She / It	was	working.
	You / We / They	were	working.
–	I / He / She / It	wasn't	working.
	You / We / They	weren't	working.
?	Was	I / he / she / it	working?
	Were	you / we / they	working?

We use the past continuous to talk about an action that was in progress in the past.

• *At 7 o'clock yesterday I was watching TV.*
• *What were you doing at 9 o'clock last night?*

We can join two past actions in one sentence. We use the simple past for a short action, and the past continuous for an action in progress when the short action happened

• *We were eating our dinner when the phone rang.*
• *When I arrived, everyone was watching a DVD.*

When and *while*

	when / while	
I was watching TV	when	*Tessa phoned me.*
Tessa phoned me	while	*I was watching TV.*

We can join two past actions with *when* or *while*.

We use *when* before the simple past.

• *She was driving home when the accident happened.*
• *When I got home, the phone was ringing.*

We use *while* before the past continuous.
• *The accident happened while she was driving home.*
• *While I was doing my homework, the phone rang.*

Transcripts

Unit 1

Page 7, Activity 8

0

BOY: That's a beautiful castle! How old is it?
GIRL: It's 970 years old.

1

GIRL: Which bus goes past your house?
BOY: Number 83.

2

GIRL: How many people are at the party?
BOY: Fred isn't here so there are 129.

3

BOY: How long is this film?
GIRL: Let me see... 98 minutes.

4

GIRL: How many pages are there in that book?
BOY: 564.

5

BOY: How long is the journey?
GIRL: 16 hours.

Page 7, Activity 9

TONY: Good morning, Mrs Smith.
MRS SMITH: Hello, Tony. How are you?
TONY: I'm fine thanks. Mrs Smith, this is my friend Sara. She's going to join my class for a few weeks.
MRS SMITH: Oh yes, hello, Sara. Nice to meet you. Welcome to our school.
SARA: Thank you.
MRS SMITH: Now, before you go to your lesson, I need some information from you. I know your first name is Sara. What's your surname?
SARA: It's Whalen.
MRS SMITH: How do you spell that?
SARA: W-H-A-L-E-N.
MRS SMITH: Thank you. And where do you come from?
SARA: I'm Canadian.
MRS SMITH: Oh, that's interesting. I'll just write that down. And how old are you Sara?
SARA: I'm thirteen.
MRS SMITH: And what's your address?
SARA: Well, I usually live on a boat, but we are staying at 25 Torrington Street for the next few weeks.
MRS SMITH: Sorry, can you say that again? 25...
SARA: Torrington Street. That's T-O-R-R-I-N-G-T-O-N.
MRS SMITH: OK. And what's your home phone number?
SARA: 5466-8907.
MRS SMITH: Can you say that more slowly please?
SARA: Oh sorry, 5466-8907.
MRS SMITH: That's fine, Sara. You can go to your class now.

Page 8, Activity 4

GARY: Hi, Maria. Did you get your new timetable?
MARIA: Yes, but I don't know where it is! Can you tell me what we're doing tomorrow?
GARY: Sure. Let's see. At ten past nine we have Maths.
MARIA: Oh no! I hope it's Geography after that at ten to ten.
GARY: I'm afraid not! It's Science – another one of your favourites!
MARIA: Great! And what have we got at ten forty-five, after the break? I think it's English...
GARY: We've got English at that time on Wednesday, but tomorrow it's Art.
MARIA: Oh, that's not too bad. And what do we have at twenty-five past eleven? Is it Sport?
GARY: It's Geography then. That's one of your favourite subjects, isn't it?
MARIA: Yeah I love it. Not like History! The teacher always gives us so much homework! Do we have that at quarter past one?
GARY: Don't worry, it's Music at that time. And then at five to two, for the last lesson of the day, we have Sport.
MARIA: Well that's a good way to end the week. Much better than Maths or History.
GARY: Yeah! Anything is better than Maths!

Unit 2

Page 10, Activity 3

SOPHIE: This is a nice photo. Is this your sister? She's really pretty.
JANE: Yeah, that's Alice. She's got long blonde hair in that photo, but it's short now.
SOPHIE: How many brothers and sisters have you got?
JANE: Two. There's Alice, and I've got a brother too. He's the little boy with fair hair. His name's Tom. He's nearly nine.
SOPHIE: When's his birthday?
JANE: Next month. I have to buy him a present.
SOPHIE: Yeah! Who's the other boy?
JANE: That's my cousin, Ben. And next to him is my uncle, Colin – the tall, thin man with long hair. He's really funny.
SOPHIE: Which one's your dad?
JANE: He's next to me. He's got brown eyes and very short hair. And he's a little fat, but Mum says he's good-looking.
SOPHIE: Where is your mum?
JANE: She's taking the photo.
SOPHIE: What does she look like?
JANE: She's got long brown hair and glasses.
SOPHIE: And are these people with white hair your grandparents?
JANE: Yeah, we don't see them very often. They live in Australia!

Page 11, Activity 8

1

GIRL: Is that your brother over there, Sam? The short one with the dark hair.

BOY: He's taller than that and his hair's long.

GIRL: Oh OK. Is that him? The one wearing glasses?

BOY: That's right. Let's go and talk to him.

2

BOY: Did your cousin stay with you this weekend, Jenny?

GIRL: She was ill so she stayed at home with my uncle.

BOY: That's a pity. Did your aunt come alone, then?

GIRL: Yes. We had a really nice time, but I did miss my cousin.

3

BOY: Is your grandfather in this photo, Sally?

GIRL: Yes, he's the one with dark hair. The woman next to him is my grandmother.

BOY: I didn't know he was so tall!

GIRL: Yes, they were both very good-looking when they were young, weren't they?

4

BOY: Have you seen the family who have just moved in next door?

GIRL: Yes, I just met them all outside. The man's a teacher and his wife is an engineer.

BOY: That's interesting. Did you talk to the children?

GIRL: I spoke to the two girls. They were very friendly. Their brother was still at school, but I hope we meet him soon.

Page 13, Activity 7

BOY: Your family have got such interesting jobs Karen. Your dad's a really good actor and your mum paints beautiful pictures.

KAREN: But that's just her hobby. She works in a school all week, teaching young children how to read and write.

BOY: And your sister's really lucky – she travels to so many different countries.

KAREN: I know. She says looking after groups of tourists is hard work. It sounds like fun to me!

BOY: And me. Your uncle works at the hospital, doesn't he?

KAREN: Mmm. I think it's hard work being a doctor. That's why he likes to paint in his free time.

BOY: Does your aunt work in the hospital too?

KAREN: Yes, she gets the food ready in the kitchens.

BOY: And your cousin – don't tell me she works there as well!

KAREN: Actually, she does. She's hoping to be a nurse, but at the moment she's got a desk job. She welcomes people and books their appointments.

BOY: Hmm. What jobs do you think we'll do when we're older?

KAREN: I don't know.

Unit 3

Page 14, Activity 3

JO: Are you free this Saturday, Sam?

SAM: Yes, I am.

JO: Great. Let's do something! How about going shopping?

SAM: That's a great idea. Where shall we meet?

JO: What about meeting outside the station at half past ten?

SAM: OK. Shall we play tennis in the afternoon?

JO: No, that sounds boring. How about going to a restaurant?

SAM: Yeah, OK. Let's try that new pizza restaurant near the station.

JO: Good idea!

Page 16, Activity 4

NICOLE: Hey, Tom.

TOM: Oh, hi, Nicole. It's your birthday party on Saturday, isn't it?

NICOLE: Yes, that's right. 7 o'clock. Don't forget!

TOM: OK! Shall I bring something to the party? Maybe some crisps?

NICOLE: Thanks, but I've got some already and Mum's bought lots of ice cream. Can you bring some drinks?

TOM: Er, I think Lisa's bringing some drinks. She's got three big bottles of cola and some fruit juice.

NICOLE: Ah, OK.

TOM: What about plates or cups?

NICOLE: Carl's bringing some paper plates. He's got lots from his birthday party last month. And Rosie is bringing some cups... Ah! I know! We've got lots of burgers, but no pizzas. Can you bring some pizza? Everyone likes pizza, right?

TOM: Sure. No problem.

NICOLE: And are you meeting Mike later?

TOM: Yeah, he's in my Maths class.

NICOLE: Great. Could you ask him to bring some music? He's got some great CDs.

TOM: Sure. Good idea.

Unit 4

Page 20, Activities 3 and 4

DAD: Hi, Liz. Have you been shopping yet?

LIZ: Yes, I went today, Dad. The shopping centre was closed yesterday and I'm busy on Tuesday.

DAD: What did you get?

LIZ: Well, I wanted a toy for my friend's baby sister. There were some picture books about animals, but in the end I bought her this ball to play with.

DAD: Very nice. Did you go to your favourite music shop?

LIZ: Yes, I listened to some pop and rock CDs and I bought this dance CD for our next party.

DAD: Great. I suppose you looked at the clothes?

LIZ: Of course. I just got a T-shirt. I tried on some jeans but they were very expensive and a great sweater

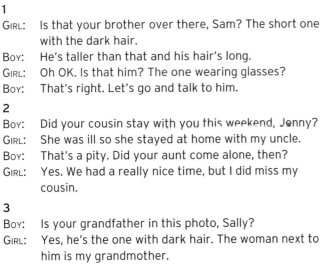

but it was too small! After that I met my friend Sally at lunchtime.

DAD: In a coffee shop?

LIZ: It was such a lovely day we decided to buy some sandwiches from a snack bar and eat them in the park.

DAD: Good idea. Did you remember my car magazine?

LIZ: I got it in a bookshop. There were none in the department store and the newsagent's was closed. There you are, Dad!

DAD: Thanks, Liz.

Page 22, Activity 4

GINA: This is my favourite room in the house. We've got lots of plants in there, so it feels like a jungle. There's a long mirror on one wall, and a large window above the bath, so lots of light comes in during the day. I love having a bath in there - it's so relaxing.

HARRY: This is my room. There's a desk with my computer on it, where I do my homework, and shelves for all my books and DVDs. And these are my drums! I've got a friend called James who plays the guitar and he often comes here to practise with me. There's a sofa in the corner, and when he needs to stay the night he sleeps on that.

DANIEL: My dad's interested in films and the cinema, so that's why we've got this room in our house! There are several big chairs in here, which are really comfortable, and soft, thick carpets on the walls and floor. There are heavy curtains in front of the screen and lots of little lights in the ceiling. We switch those off when we watch a film.

Unit 5

Page 24, Activity 4

Good afternoon everyone and welcome to the show! Today we are going to cook minestrone. It's a really wonderful soup, and so easy to make! The first thing to do is to put some water into a pan. To make soup for four people you will need about 2 litres of water.

The next thing to do is to cut some vegetables into small pieces. It doesn't really matter what kind of vegetables you use, just look in the fridge and see what you've got. Today, I'm going to use one onion, one carrot, one potato and some green vegetables.

When everything is ready, fry the onion, carrot and potato in some oil. I usually do this for about five minutes. Then put them into the water and let them boil. After about ten minutes, add the green vegetables and some pasta. I usually use 200 grams. When everything is soft, add some salt and pepper. Finally, put the soup into a bowl, put some cheese on top and it's ready to eat!

Page 27, Activities 5 and 6

WAITER: Hi. Are you ready to order?

MIKE: Yes. I'd like a cheeseburger, please.

WAITER: OK.

MIKE: Would you like a burger too, Amy?

AMY: No, I don't eat meat. Can I have a pizza please, with tomato, cheese, onions and peppers?

WAITER: Sure. Do you want any side dishes with that?

AMY: I'll have some onion rings.

MIKE: And I'll have a salad.

WAITER: What about a dessert afterwards?

AMY: Can I have some banana cake?

MIKE: And a chocolate brownie for me, please.

WAITER: Right. Would you like something to drink?

MIKE: Can I just have a glass of water, please?

WAITER: No problem.

AMY: And I'd like a glass of lemonade.

WAITER: OK. It won't be long.

MIKE: Thanks.

Unit 6

Page 30, Activities 4 and 5

WOMAN: Hello, Dave Martin's School of Rock. How can I help you?

BOY: Oh hello. I saw your advertisement in the newspaper and I'm ringing to ask about the guitar lessons on Fridays and Saturdays.

WOMAN: Actually, it's drum lessons on Fridays. But we're starting a group guitar course on Saturday mornings. Can you play the guitar already?

BOY: No, I'm a beginner.

WOMAN: OK, well, you need to come at 9.30 then. The class at 10.30 is a higher level.

BOY: How many people will there be in the class?

WOMAN: Well, there will never be more than 12, but we must have six, or we will close the class, I'm afraid.

BOY: And how much are the classes?

WOMAN: Well, our usual price is £35.00 an hour, but because it's a group it will only be £17.50 a lesson. That means it's £175.00 for the term.

BOY: That sounds fine. When does the course begin?

WOMAN: The first lesson is on the 7th of March. But you need to come and fill in the booking form on the 3rd.

BOY: Fine. I'll do that. Thanks very much.

Unit 7

Page 35, Activity 6

For a fun day out for the family, how about taking a trip to the Museum of Fashion in the city of Bath this weekend?

The museum shows how fashions have changed over the last four centuries and each of the 12 rooms has clothes from different times. Kids will love the mini-skirts and platform shoes from the 1960s!

This month there is a special exhibition of dresses that visitors can actually try on. These are from the 18th and 19th century so remember to bring your camera!

The museum is open from 10 o'clock until 5 o'clock on weekdays and until half past five on Saturdays and Sundays. Entrance costs £7 for adults and £5 for children under sixteen. There's also a special family ticket for £20 that covers two adults and up to four children.

If you're coming by car, the best place to park is in Charlotte Street, that's C-H-A-R-L-O-double T-E, and just follow the signs.

Unit 8

Page 38, Activity 2

1

DOCTOR: What's wrong?

BOY: I feel really sick and my stomach hurts!

DOCTOR: It might be something you ate. You should rest and drink some water.

2

DOCTOR: What's the matter?

GIRL: I've got a terrible pain in my ear.

DOCTOR: It looks very red. You should take this medicine three times a day.

3

BOY A: Are you OK?

BOY B: I had an accident when I was cycling to school.

BOY A: You should go to hospital for an X-ray. Your arm may be broken.

4

TEACHER: What's the matter?

GIRL: I don't feel very well. I've got a temperature and a headache.

TEACHER: Why don't you go home and rest? You might have the flu.

Unit 9

Page 45, Activity 7

1

WOMAN: It's too windy for cycling. Let's just go for a walk today.

MAN: But this weather's great for sailing – let's do that.

WOMAN: OK and we can do the bike ride tomorrow. I heard on the TV that the wind's going to stop tonight.

MAN: Good idea!

2

GIRL: I hope you have lots of snow on your skiing holiday.

BOY: Thanks, but I've just heard the weather forecast and it's not at all good.

GIRL: It's not going to rain, is it?

BOY: Worse than that – it's going to be warm and sunny, so there won't be any snow!

3

MAN: Thanks for the postcard. Could you see those mountains from your hotel window?

WOMAN: They were behind the hotel. Our room was at the front and we were very near the sea.

MAN: So could you see the beach?

WOMAN: It was too far away. But we could see the fishing boats really well – it was very interesting.

4

BOY: Sorry I'm late.

TEACHER: Did your dad have problems with the car again?

BOY: The car's fine. But there was a big tree across the road near our house – I think it fell down in that terrible thunderstorm during the night – so I had to walk and it took a long time

TEACHER: Oh well. Never mind!

Unit 10

Page 49, Activity 6

Now listen carefully everyone – here are our plans for tomorrow. Breakfast will be at 8 o'clock. Don't be late because we're going on to the London Eye at nine thirty and it will take us 40 minutes to get there. A ride on the London Eye takes 30 minutes and if the weather's good, we'll get a great view of the city.

Next, we're walking to Covent Garden. At twelve thirty we'll have lunch and then you can do some shopping. Lunch will cost about £10 and you'll need some spending money as well. £20 will be enough I think.

At 3 o'clock we're going to the Science Museum. We're seeing a film there called *Deep Sea* in the 3D cinema. You won't believe your eyes when you see some of the fish in that film!

After that, at about six, we're going back to the hotel to have dinner. There will also be time for you to have a rest and change your clothes.

Finally, at seven thirty we are going to see Grease at the Piccadilly Theatre. That's P-I-C-C-A-D-I-L-L-Y. It's a great show and I'm sure you will all really enjoy it.

Page 51, Activity 6

ANDY: Hi, Teresa. How was your holiday in the US?

TERESA: It was great, but six weeks wasn't enough. We needed another three or four weeks!

ANDY: Did you travel around by car?

TERESA: Most people do that, but we went everywhere by bus. The trains are good too, but we didn't use those.

ANDY: Did you go to Disneyland?

TERESA: Yeah! I couldn't believe how big it was. And we were lucky because it wasn't very busy the day we went. But Mum and Dad weren't happy about the prices!

ANDY: And what about the Grand Canyon?

TERESA: That was great! Some people take a helicopter or a plane flight to see it, but we did it the hard way – on foot!

ANDY: And did you visit any interesting towns?

TERESA: Lots! Los Angeles, San Francisco, Las Vegas. We also wanted to go to Phoenix but there wasn't enough time.

ANDY: What did you think of San Francisco?

TERESA: We loved it – my mum liked the cafés and restaurants and I liked the zoo. Dad liked the bridge best.

ANDY: It sounds like an amazing holiday!

TERESA: It was!

Unit 11

Page 52, Activity 2

LIZ: So what is there to do in Hadley, Tina?

TINA: Well, we've got a castle from the 13th century.

LIZ: Hmm. I'm not too interested in ruins. But I love swimming.

TINA: Me too. I went to the new pool in the sports centre last week. It's really big.

LIZ: Sounds great. Do you have a movie theatre here?

TINA: Yes. And there's a good film on this week. It's called *The Tale of Despereaux*. Have you seen it?

LIZ: No. What's it called again? *The Tale of...*

TINA: *Despereaux*. That's D-E-S-P-E-R-E-A-U-X. I haven't seen it either. Shall we go?

LIZ: Sure.

TINA: During the week is best. Tickets are only £4.50 then. On Saturdays and Sundays they're £7.50.

LIZ: OK! Is there a skatepark?

TINA: Yes, it's across the road from the library, by the river, but I've never been there.

LIZ: Great. Oh I nearly forgot – I've just written a postcard to my mom and dad but I haven't mailed it yet.

TINA: You'll have to hurry. The post office shuts at half past five and it's quarter past five already.

LIZ: Sounds like I don't have time – I'll go tomorrow.

Page 54, Activity 2

1

BOY: Excuse me, where's the post office?

GIRL: The post office? Go straight on past the church, and then take the first road on the left. The post office is at the end of that road, next to the river.

BOY: Take the first road on the left. OK. Is it far?

GIRL: About two minutes on foot.

BOY: Thanks.

2

GIRL: Can you help me? I'm looking for The Orange House.

BOY: That's the dance club, isn't it? Go straight on and turn left at the traffic lights.

GIRL: Is it on the other side of the river?

BOY: No, if you go over the bridge you've gone too far. It's opposite the post office. You can't miss it.

GIRL: OK, thanks.

3

BOY: Excuse me, is there a supermarket near here?

GIRL: Yes, but it's quite far. Go straight on and turn right at the traffic lights. Go past the museum and the hotel until you get to the big roundabout. Turn left at the roundabout and left again at the traffic lights. The supermarket's on the right, opposite the library.

BOY: So right at the traffic lights, then left at the roundabout and left again. Great. Thanks a lot.

GIRL: No problem.

Unit 12

Page 56, Activity 4

PRESENTER: And the next caller on the line is Annie. Hi, Annie. Do you think you are addicted to modern technology?

ANNIE: Well, my mum says I am, but I don't agree. I probably spend about two hours a day online, chatting to friends or looking at websites, and I send about 60 text messages a day. I don't think that's a lot, do you?

PRESENTER: It sounds like a lot to me! When do you send all those texts?

ANNIE: Between lessons and after school. But my teacher took my phone away yesterday. I hope he gives it back to me soon! I want to know what my friends are doing.

PRESENTER: But you shouldn't use your phone during lessons!

ANNIE: I know. But I wasn't sending text messages; I was trying to find some information on the internet!

PRESENTER: I see! So, Annie, why do you think adults worry about teenagers and the way they use modern technology?

ANNIE: I don't know! They worry too much. They think it's bad for us, but it isn't. It helps us study and it helps us stay in touch with our friends!

PRESENTER: OK. Thanks, Annie. And our next caller is...

Exam Guide

Listening Part 1

0

GIRL: Were there many people at the party last night?

BOY: About 30.

GIRL: That's not many.

BOY: No, but more than last time.

1

PHILLIP: Have you done your history project, Lizzie? Don't we have to give it to the teacher on Monday? I haven't started mine yet!

LIZZIE: Don't worry, we've got more time than that. She doesn't want it until Friday now.

PHILLIP: Really? When did she tell us that?

LIZZIE: In the lesson on Wednesday. Weren't you listening, Phillip?

2

MUM: Do you need anything for the holiday, Melissa? Have you got enough T-shirts?

MELISSA: I've got lots of T-shirts, Mum, but I can't find my sunglasses anywhere.

MUM: They're in the cupboard in my bedroom. What about shorts? I'm sure yours are all too small for you now.

MELISSA: You're right. Let's get some new ones when we go shopping tomorrow.

3

BOY: What time shall we go to the basketball match on Sunday, James?

JAMES: Well, it starts at a quarter to two, so I think we should try to be there at a quarter past one.
BOY: OK. I'll see you at the bus stop at twelve forty-five.
JAMES: Fine. Don't be late!

4
BOY: Do you live on Farley Street, Sandra?
SANDRA: That's right. Number 14, next to the house with the big gates.
BOY: Oh, I know. There's a tree in your front garden, isn't there?
SANDRA: That's number 18. We've got flowers in our front garden. My mum loves growing things!

5
BOY A: Let's play one of your computer games. This car racing one looks good.
BOY B: I'm a bit bored with that. Let me show you this one. You make songs with it. It's really clever.
BOY A: OK. And when you come to my house we can play with my new football one.
BOY B: Great! I really like football games.

Listening Part 2

TIM: Hi, Mia. How was school?
MIA: Hi, Tim. Good. We did a class project to find out people's favourite TV programmes. There were some surprises.
TIM: I know what you like best – cartoons!
MIA: That's right. And everyone knows Rob loves anything to do with plants and animals.
TIM: Your friend Hannah's a great cook, she must watch all the cooking shows.
MIA: You're wrong. She's a big fan of rock and reggae so she loves any concerts on TV.
TIM: Carl really likes tennis so I suppose he likes sports programmes best.
MIA: He prefers playing to watching. But he never misses anything about foreign countries and places to go on holiday.
TIM: And what about Rosie? She's very clever, isn't she?
MIA: Her favourite shows are the ones where teams answer questions and win prizes – she says she learns a lot from them. Anyway, what programmes do you like best, Tim?
TIM: Oh I really enjoy an exciting film – for me that's even better than an international football match.

Listening Part 3

FELICITY: Hi, Daniel. I missed yesterday's meeting about the school camping trip. Are we still going on the 15th of May?
DANIEL: We leave on the 29th now, Felicity. But we have to pay by the 22nd.
FELICITY: OK. How much is it?
DANIEL: It's £55 for the campsite and £27 for the food, so it's £82 all together.
FELICITY: That's not bad. What do we have to bring?
DANIEL: Well, the campsite has tents for us, but we need our own sleeping bags. We can use the school's plates and cups.
FELICITY: Where are we going? To the mountains again?
DANIEL: To the south coast this year. The campsite's on a farm but the beach is only ten minutes away by bus.
FELICITY: That sounds great! And what are we going to do there?
DANIEL: Well, swimming and windsurfing, of course. And some climbing if the weather's good. But there won't be any long walks this year.
FELICITY: Oh good! And I suppose we have to leave really early?
DANIEL: That's right! It takes six hours to get there, so the coach is leaving at six thirty. We have to meet at school at a quarter past six.
FELICITY: Oh no!

Listening Part 4

ROS: Why don't you come to the Art Club at the museum on Saturday, Dan?
DAN: Oh, I don't know...
ROS: You won't have to get up early. It starts at ten thirty and it finishes at half past twelve. It's really good fun.
DAN: But you know I'm no good at painting.
ROS: That doesn't matter. Last week we made animals out of card, and next time we're making posters to put on the wall.
DAN: Is it expensive?
ROS: My mum booked five meetings for me and she paid £12.50, but it's £3.50 if you just go to one.
DAN: OK. I'll come! Which room is it in the museum?
ROS: In the library, on the ground floor just past the café.
DAN: I know. Do I need to take anything with me?
ROS: One week we had to take a bottle to draw, but this week you'll only need an old shirt to keep you clean.
DAN: I'm sure Dad's got one. See you Saturday!

Listening Part 5

Hi, Charlie. It's Graham. I'm just calling about going to the cinema tomorrow. The film is on at the Apex Cinema on Tillbury Road, that's T-I-L-L-B-U-R-Y. Do you know where it is? I think there's a map on their website. The tickets there are usually £5.70 but ours will only be £4.50 because we're going in the afternoon. I'm going to take some extra money as well, so I can get some popcorn. The film starts at four thirty, but let's meet at 3 o'clock. I want to show you the photos from skateboarding at the weekend. They're really good! So, where shall we meet? I think there's a restaurant on one side of the cinema, but it's quite expensive. I'll wait for you in the café on the other side. We can look at my photos there. Anyway, my mobile is 07869-345211. Call me if there's a problem. See you!

KET for schools Vocabulary list

Unit 1

Countries

Argentina	n	/ɑːdʒən'tiːnə/ (AmE /ɑːrdʒən'tiːnə/)
Australia	n	/ɒ'streɪliə/
Brazil	n	/brə'zɪl/
Canada	n	/'kænədə/
China	n	/'tʃaɪnə/
Greece	n	/griːs/
Ireland	n	/'aɪələnd/ (AmE /'aɪərlənd/)
Mexico	n	/'meksɪkəʊ/
Poland	n	/'pəʊlənd/
Spain	n	/speɪn/
Thailand	n	/'taɪlænd/

Languages

Chinese	n	/tʃaɪ'niːz/
English	n	/'ɪŋglɪʃ/
French	n	/frentʃ/
Greek	n	/griːk/
Italian	n	/ɪ'tæliən/
Polish	n	/'pəʊlɪʃ/
Portuguese	n	/pɔːtjuˈgiːz/ (AmE /pɔːrtjuˈgiːz/)
Spanish	n	/'spænɪʃ/
Thai	n	/taɪ/

Nationalities

Argentinian	adj	/ɑːdʒən'tɪniən/ (AmE /ɑːrdʒən'tɪniən/)
Australian	adj	/ɒ'streɪliən/
Brazilian	adj	/brə'zɪliən/
Canadian	adj	/kə'neɪdiən/
Chinese	adj	/tʃaɪ'niːz/
Greek	adj	/griːk/
Irish	adj	/'aɪərɪʃ/
Italian	adj	/ɪ'tæliən/
Mexican	adj	/'meksɪkən/
Polish	adj	/'pəʊlɪʃ/
Spanish	adj	/'spænɪʃ/
Thai	adj	/taɪ/

Numbers

one		/wʌn/
two		/tuː/
three		/θriː/
four		/fɔː(r)/
five		/faɪv/
six		/'sɪks/
seven		/'sevn/
eight		/eɪt/
nine		/naɪn/
ten		/ten/
eleven		/ɪ'levn/
twelve		/twelv/
thirteen		/θɜː'tiːn/ (AmE /θɜːr'tiːn/)
fourteen		/fɔː'tiːn/ (AmE /fɔːr'tiːn/)
fifteen		/fɪf'tiːn/
sixteen		/sɪks'tiːn/
seventeen		/sevn'tiːn/
eighteen		/eɪ'tiːn/
nineteen		/naɪn'tiːn/
twenty		/'twenti/

thirty		/'θɜːti/ (AmE /'θɜːrti/)
forty		/'fɔːti/ (AmE /'fɔːrti/)
fifty		/'fɪfti/
sixty		/'sɪksti/
seventy		/'sevnti/
eighty		/'eɪti/
ninety		/'naɪnti/
a hundred		/ə 'hʌndrəd/

Personal details

address	n	/ə'dres/ (AmE /'ædres/)
age	n	/eɪdʒ/
country	n	/'kʌntri/
favourite (AmE favorite)	adj	/'feɪvərɪt/
first name	n	/'fɜːst neɪm/ (AmE /'fɜːrst neɪm/)
name	n	/neɪm/
number	n	/'nʌmbə(r)/
phone number	n	/'fəʊn 'nʌmbə(r)/
street	n	/striːt/
surname	n	/'sɜːneɪm/ (AmE /'sɜːrneɪm/)
... years old		/jɪəz 'əʊld/ (AmE /jɪərz 'əʊld/)

Days

birthday	n	/'bɜːθdeɪ/ (AmE /'bɜːrθdeɪ/)
Monday	n	/'mʌndeɪ/
Tuesday	n	/'tjuːzdeɪ/ (AmE /'tuːzdeɪ/)
Wednesday	n	/'wenzdeɪ/
Thursday	n	/'θɜːzdeɪ/ (AmE /'θɜːrzdeɪ/)
Friday	n	/'fraɪdeɪ/
Saturday	n	/'sætədeɪ/ (AmE /'sætərdeɪ/)
Sunday	n	/'sʌndeɪ/
weekday	n	/'wiːkdeɪ/
weekend	n	/wiːk'end/

Times

half past		/'hɑːf 'pɑːst/
a quarter past (AmE a quarter after)		/ə 'kwɔːtə pɑːst/ (AmE /ə 'kwɔːrtər æftər/)
a quarter to (AmE a quarter of)		/ə 'kwɔːtə tu/ (AmE /ə 'kwɔːrtər ɒv/)

School subjects

Art	n	/ɑːt/ (AmE /ɑːrt/)
Computer studies	n	/kəm'pjuːtə 'stʌdiz/ (AmE /kəm'pjuːtər 'stʌdiz/)
Design	n	/dɪ'zaɪn/
Drama	n	/'drɑːmə/
English	n	/'ɪŋglɪʃ/
French	n	/frentʃ/
Geography	n	/dʒi'ɒgrəfi/
History	n	/'hɪstri/
Maths (AmE Math)	n	/mæθs/ (AmE /mæθ/)
Science	n	/'saɪəns/
Sports	n	/spɔːts/ (AmE /spɔːrts/)

School words

break	n	/breɪk/
course	n	/kɔːs/ (AmE /kɔːrs/)
homework	n	/'həʊmwɜːk/ (AmE /'həʊmwɜːrk/)
lesson	n	/'lesn/
student	n	/'stjuːdnt/ (AmE /'stuːdnt/)
subject	n	/'sʌbjekt/
timetable	n	/'taɪmteɪbl/

Unit 2

The family

aunt	n	/ɑːnt/ (AmE /ænt/)
boy	n	/bɔɪ/
brother	n	/ˈbrʌðə(r)/
child, children	n	/tʃaɪld/, /ˈtʃɪldrən /
cousin	n	/ˈkʌzn/
dad	n	/dæd/
daughter	n	/ˈdɔːtə(r)/
family	n	/ˈfæməli/
father	n	/ˈfɑːðə(r)/
friend	n	/frend/
girl	n	/gɜːl/ (AmE /gɜːrl/)
granddad	n	/ˈgrændæd /
grandfather	n	/ˈgrænfɑːðə(r)/
grandma	n	/ˈgrænmɑː/
grandmother	n	/ˈgrænmʌðə(r)/
husband	n	/ˈhʌzbənd/
mother	n	/ˈmʌðə(r)/
mum	n	/mʌm/
parents	n	/ˈpeərənts/
pet	n	/pet/
sister	n	/ˈsɪstə(r)/
son	n	/sʌn/
uncle	n	/ˈʌŋkl/
wife	n	/waɪf/

Describing people

beautiful	adj	/ˈbjuːtɪfl/
black	adj	/blæk/
blonde	adj	/blɒnd/
blue	adj	/bluː/
brown	adj	/braʊn/
dark	adj	/dɑːk/ (AmE /dɑːrk/)
eyes	n	/aɪz/
fair	adj	/feə(r)/
fat	adj	/fæt/
green	adj	/griːn/
grey (AmE gray)	adj	/greɪ/
hair	n	/heə(r)/
long	adj	/lɒŋ/
look like	v	/ˈlʊk ˈlaɪk/
old	adj	/əʊld/
pretty	adj	/ˈprɪti/
red	adj	/red/
short	adj	/ʃɔːt/
tall	adj	/tɔːl/
thin	adj	/θɪn/
white	adj	/waɪt/
young	adj	/jʌŋ/

Jobs

builder	n	/ˈbɪldə(r)/
dentist	n	/ˈdentɪst/
doctor	n	/ˈdɒktə(r)/
farmer	n	/ˈfɑːmə(r)/ (AmE /ˈfɑːrmə(r)/)
gardener	n	/ˈgɑːdnə(r)/ (AmE /ˈgɑːrdnə(r)/)
hairdresser	n	/ˈheədresə(r)/ (AmE /ˈheərdresə(r)/)
journalist	n	/ˈdʒɜːnəlɪst/ (AmE /ˈdʒɜːrnəlɪst/)
mechanic	n	/məˈkænɪk/
nurse	n	/nɜːs/ (AmE /nɜːrs/)
painter	n	/ˈpeɪntə(r)/
pilot	n	/ˈpaɪlət/
police officer	n	/pəˈliːs ˈɒfɪsə(r)/
teacher	n	/ˈtiːtʃə(r)/
actor	n	/ˈæktə(r)/
cook	n	/kʊk/
receptionist	n	/rɪˈsepʃənɪst/
tour guide	n	/ˈtʊə(r) gaɪd/

Words describing jobs

boring	adj	/ˈbɔːrɪŋ/
difficult	adj	/ˈdɪfɪkəlt/
dirty	adj	/ˈdɜːti/ (AmE /ˈdɜːrti/)
exciting	adj	/ɪkˈsaɪtɪŋ/
interesting	adj	/ˈɪntrestɪŋ/
scary	adj	/ˈskeəri/
tiring	adj	/ˈtaɪrɪŋ/

Jobs verbs

build	v	/bɪld/
check	v	/tʃek/
drive	v	/draɪv/
fly	v	/flaɪ/
grow	v	/grəʊ/
keep	v	/kiːp/
look after	v	/lʊk ˈɑːftə(r)/ (AmE /lʊk ˈæftər/)
paint	v	/peɪnt/
repair	v	/rɪˈpeə(r)/
teach	v	/tiːtʃ/
work	v	/wɜːk/ (AmE /wɜːrk/)
write	v	/raɪt/

Unit 3

Free time activities

baseball	n	/ˈbeɪsbɔːl/
beach	n	/biːtʃ/
café	n	/ˈkæfeɪ/ (AmE /kæˈfeɪ/)
cinema (AmE movie theater)	n	/ˈsɪnəmə/ (AmE /ˈmuːvi θɪətər/)
computer games	n	/kəmˈpjuːtə geɪmz/ (AmE /kəmˈpjuːtər geɪmz/)
DVD	n	/diː viː ˈdiː/
football match (AmE soccer match)	n	/ˈfʊtbɔːl mætʃ/ (AmE /ˈsɒkər mætʃ/)
film (AmE movie)	n	/fɪlm/ (AmE /ˈmuːvi/)
restaurant	n	/ˈrestrɒnt/
running	n	/ˈrʌnɪŋ/
shopping	n	/ˈʃɒpɪŋ/
surfing	n	/ˈsɜːfɪŋ/ (AmE /ˈsɜːrfɪŋ/)
swimming	n	/ˈswɪmɪŋ/
tennis	n	/ˈtenɪs/
television	n	/ˈtelɪvɪʒn/
meet	v	/miːt/
pool	n	/puːl/
ticket	n	/ˈtɪkɪt/

Party things

balloon	n	/bəˈluːn/
barbecue	n	/ˈbɑːbɪkjuː/ (AmE /ˈbɑːrbɪkjuː/)
burger	n	/ˈbɜːgə(r)/ (AmE /ˈbɜːrgər/)
cake	n	/keɪk/
candle	n	/ˈkændl/
card	n	/kɑːd/ (AmE /kɑːrd/)
CD	n	/siː ˈdiː/
chicken	n	/ˈtʃɪkɪn/
crisps	n	/krɪsps/
cup	n	/kʌp/
disco	n	/ˈdɪskəʊ/
drink	n	/drɪŋk/
fruit juice	n	/ˈfruːt dʒuːs/

glass	n	/glɑːs/ (AmE /glæs/)
ice cream	n	/ˈaɪs kriːm/
pizza	n	/ˈpiːtsə/
plate	n	/pleɪt/
present	n	/ˈpreznt/
bring	v	/brɪŋ/
invitation	n	/ɪnvɪˈteɪʃn/
meat	n	/miːt/
music	n	/ˈmjuːzɪk/
orange juice	n	/ˈɒrɪndʒ dʒuːs/
sandwich	n	/ˈsænwɪtʃ/

Unit 4

Shops		
bookshop	n	/ˈbʊkʃɒp/
clothes shop	n	/ˈkləʊðz ʃɒp/
coffee shop	n	/ˈkɒfi ʃɒp/
department store	n	/dɪˈpɑːtmənt stɔː(r)/ (AmE /dɪˈpɑːrtmənt stɔːr/)
music shop	n	/ˈmjuːzɪk ʃɒp/
newsagent's	n	/ˈnjuːzeɪdʒənts/
snack bar	n	/ˈsnæk bɑː(r)/
sports shop	n	/ˈspɔːts ʃɒp/ (AmE /ˈspɔːrts ʃɒp/)
supermarket	n	/ˈsuːpəmɑːkɪt/ (AmE /ˈsuːpərmɑːrkɪt/)
toyshop	n	/ˈtɔɪ ʃɒp/
shopping centre (AmE shopping mall)	n	/ˈʃɒpɪŋ sentə(r)/ (AmE /ˈʃɒpɪŋ mɔːl/)

Things you buy		
ball	n	/bɔːl/
book	n	/bʊk/
comic book	n	/ˈkɒmɪk bʊk/
football shirt (AmE soccer shirt))	n	/ˈfʊtbɔːl ʃɜːt/ (AmE /ˈsɒkər ʃɜːrt/)
magazine	n	/mægəˈziːn/ (AmE /ˈmægəziːn/)
makeup	n	/ˈmeɪkʌp/
mobile phone	n	/məʊbaɪl ˈfəʊn/
sweets (AmE candies)	n	/swiːts/ (AmE /ˈkændiz/)
trainers (AmE sneakers)	n	/ˈtreɪnəz/ (AmE /ˈsniːkərz/)

Shopping words		
assistant	n	/əˈsɪstənt/
buy	v	/baɪ/
how much?		/haʊ ˈmʌtʃ/
lift (AmE elevator)	n	/lɪft/ (AmE /ˈeləveɪtər/)
price	n	/praɪs/
spend	v	/spend/

The home		
apartment	n	/əˈpɑːtmənt/ (AmE /əˈpɑːrtmənt/)
bathroom	n	/ˈbɑːθruːm/ (AmE /ˈbæθruːm/)
bedroom	n	/ˈbedruːm/
dining room	n	/ˈdaɪnɪŋ ruːm/
flat (AmE apartment)	n	/flæt/ (AmE /əˈpɑːrtmənt/)
garden (AmE yard)	n	/ˈgɑːdən/ (AmE /ˈjɑːrd/)
garage	n	/ˈgærɑːʒ/ (AmE /gəˈrɑːʒ/)
hall	n	/hɔːl/
home	n	/həʊm/
house	n	/haʊs/
kitchen	n	/ˈkɪtʃɪn/
living room	n	/ˈlɪvɪŋ ruːm/

Furniture and things in the home		
bath	n	/ˈbɑːθ/ (AmE /bæθ/)
bed	n	/bed/

bookcase	n	/ˈbʊkeɪs /
carpet	n	/ˈkɑːpɪt/ (AmE /ˈkɑːrpɪt/)
ceiling	n	/ˈsiːlɪŋ/
chair	n	/tʃeə(r)/
computer	n	/kɒmˈpjuːtə(r)/
cupboard	n	/ˈkʌbəd/ (AmE /ˈkʌbərd/)
curtain	n	/ˈkɜːtən/ (AmE /ˈkɜːrtən/)
desk	n	/desk/
door	n	/dɔː(r)/
floor	n	/flɔː(r)/
lamp	n	/læmp/
light	n	/laɪt/
pillow	n	/ˈpɪləʊ/
poster	n	/ˈpəʊstə(r)/
shelf	n	/ʃelf/
shower	n	/ˈʃaʊə(r)/
sink	n	/sɪŋk/
sofa	n	/ˈsəʊfə/
toilet (AmE bathroom)	n	/ˈtɔɪlət/ (AmE /ˈbæθruːm/)
towel	n	/ˈtaʊəl/
TV	n	/tiː ˈviː/
wall	n	/wɔːl/
window	n	/ˈwɪndəʊ/

Unit 5

Food		
apple	n	/ˈæpl/
banana	n	/bəˈnɑːnə/ (AmE /bəˈnænə/)
butter	n	/ˈbʌtə(r)/
carrot	n	/ˈkærət/
cereal	n	/ˈsɪəriəl/
cheese	n	/tʃiːz/
chips	n	/tʃɪps/
chocolate	n	/ˈtʃɒklət/
coffee	n	/ˈkɒfi/
egg	n	/eg/
grapes	n	/greɪps/
jam	n	/dʒæm/
lemon	n	/ˈlemən/
mango	n	/ˈmæŋgəʊ/
milk	n	/mɪlk/
onion	n	/ˈʌnjən/
oil	n	/ɔɪl/
pasta	n	/ˈpæstə/
pepper	n	/ˈpepə(r)/
pineapple	n	/ˈpaɪnæpl/
potato	n	/pəˈteɪtəʊ/
rice	n	/raɪs/
salad	n	/ˈsæləd/
salt	n	/sɒlt/
steak	n	/steɪk/
sugar	n	/ˈʃʊgə(r)/
tea	n	/tiː/
biscuit (AmE cookie)	n	/ˈbɪskɪt/ (AmE /ˈkʊki/)
soup	n	/suːp/
vegetable	n	/ˈvedʒtəbl/

Containers		
bottle	n	/ˈbɒtl/
bowl	n	/bəʊl/
box	n	/bɒks/
can	n	/kæn/
glass	n	/glɑːs/ (AmE /glæs/)

Menus		
dessert	n	/dɪˈzɜːt/ (AmE /dɪˈzɜːrt/)
drink	n	/drɪŋk/
main course	n	/ˈmeɪn kɔːs/ (AmE /ˈmeɪn kɔːrs/)
side dish	n	/ˈsaɪd dɪʃ/
waiter	n	/ˈweɪtə(r)/

Unit 6

Films		
action film (AmE action movie)	n	/ˈækʃən fɪlm/ (AmE /ˈækʃən muːvi/)
adventure film (AmE adventure movie)	n	/ədˈventʃə fɪlm/ (AmE /ədˈventʃə(r) muːvi/)
comedy	n	/ˈkɒmədi/
fantasy	n	/ˈfæntəsi/
horror film (AmE horror movie)	n	/ˈhɒrə fɪlm/ (AmE /ˈhɒrər muːvi/)
romance	n	/ˈrəʊmæns/
science fiction film (AmE science fiction movie)	n	/saɪəns ˈfɪkʃən fɪlm/ (AmE /saɪəns ˈfɪkʃən muːvi/)
thriller	n	/ˈθrɪlə(r)/

Words for describing films		
boring	adj	/ˈbɔːrɪŋ/
exciting	adj	/ɪkˈsaɪtɪŋ/
funny	adj	/ˈfʌni/
interesting	adj	/ˈɪntrestɪŋ/
sad	adj	/sæd/
scary	adj	/ˈskeəri/
strange	adj	/streɪndʒ/
terrible	adj	/ˈterəbl/
wonderful	adj	/ˈwʌndəfʊl/ (AmE /ˈwʌndərfʊl/)

Verbs		
cry	v	/kraɪ/
laugh	v	/lɑːf/ (AmE /læf/)
smile	v	/smaɪl/

Entertainment words		
band	n	/bænd/
famous	adj	/ˈfeɪməs/
guitar	n	/ɡɪˈtɑː(r)/
listen	v	/ˈlɪsn/
play	n	/pleɪ/
see	v	/siː/
watch	v	/wɒtʃ/

Kinds of music		
classical	adj	/ˈklæsɪkl/
dance	n	/dɑːns/ (AmE /dæns/)
hip hop	n	/ˈhɪp hɒp/
pop	n	/pɒp/
reggae	n	/ˈreɡeɪ/
rock	n	/rɒk/

Musical instruments		
drums	n	/drʌmz/
electric guitar	n	/ɪˈlektrɪk ɡɪˈtɑː(r)/
instrument	n	/ˈɪnstrəmənt/
keyboard	n	/ˈkiːbɔːd/ (AmE /ˈkiːbɔːrd/)
piano	n	/piˈænəʊ/
violin	n	/vaɪəˈlɪn/

Unit 7

Clothes		
bag	n	/bæg/
belt	n	/belt/
boots	n	/buːts/
cap	n	/kæp/

coat	n	/kəʊt/
dress	n	/dres/
jacket	n	/ˈdʒækɪt/
jeans	n	/dʒiːnz/
leather	adj	/ˈleðə(r)/
pair	n	/peə(r)/
put on	v	/pʊt ˈɒn/
shirt	n	/ʃɜːt/ (AmE /ʃɜːrt/)
shoes	n	/ʃuːz/
shorts	n	/ʃɔːts/ (AmE /ʃɔːrts/)
skirt	n	/skɜːt/ (AmE /skɜːrt/)
socks	n	/sɒks/
suit	n	/suːt/
sunglasses	n	/ˈsʌnglɑːsɪz/ (AmE /ˈsʌnglæsɪz/)
sweater	n	/ˈswetə(r)/
tie	n	/taɪ/
top	n	/tɒp/
trainers (AmE sneakers)	n	/ˈtreɪnəz/ (AmE /ˈsniːkərz/)
trousers (AmE pants)	n	/ˈtraʊzəz/ (AmE /pænts/)
T-shirt	n	/ˈtiː ʃɜːt/ (AmE /ˈtiː ʃɜːrt/)
uniform	n	/ˈjuːnɪfɔːm/ (AmE /ˈjuːnɪfɔːrm/)
wear	v	/weə(r)/

Festivals		
band	n	/bænd/
costume	n	/ˈkɒstjuːm/
crowd	n	/kraʊd/
dancer	n	/ˈdɑːnsə(r)/
drum	n	/drʌm/
festival	n	/ˈfestɪvəl/
food	n	/fuːd/
head-dress	n	/ˈheddres/
lorry (AmE truck)	n	/ˈlɒri/ (AmE /trʌk/)
parade	n	/pəˈreɪd/
clown	n	/klaʊn/
gold	adj	/ɡəʊld/
silver	adj	/ˈsɪlvə(r)/

Unit 8

Parts of the body		
arm	n	/ɑːm/ (AmE /ɑːrm/)
back	n	/bæk/
ear	n	/ɪə(r)/
eye	n	/aɪ/
face	n	/feɪs/
foot	n	/fʊt/
hand	n	/hænd/
head	n	/hed/
leg	n	/leɡ/
mouth	n	/maʊθ/
neck	n	/nek/
nose	n	/nəʊz/
stomach	n	/ˈstʌmək/
tooth	n	/tuːθ/

Health problems		
accident	n	/ˈæksɪdənt/
broken	adj	/ˈbrəʊkən/
cold	n	/kəʊld/
flu	n	/fluː/
headache	n	/ˈhedeɪk/
hospital	n	/ˈhɒspɪtl/
hurt	v	/hɜːt/ (AmE /hɜːrt/)
medicine	n	/ˈmedɪsn/

pain	n	/peɪn/
rest	v	/rest/
sick	adj	/sɪk/
sunburn	n	/'sʌnbɜːn/ (AmE /'sʌnbɜːrn/)
temperature	n	/'temprətʃə(r)/
well	adj	/wel/
What's the matter?		/wɒts ðə 'mætə(r)/
What's wrong?		/wɒts 'rɒŋ/

Sports

baseball	n	/'beɪsbɔːl/
basketball	n	/'bɑːskɪtbɔːl/ (AmE /'bæskɪtbɔːl/)
climbing	n	/'klaɪmɪŋ/
fishing	n	/'fɪʃɪŋ/
football (AmE soccer)	n	/'fʊtbɔːl/ (AmE /'sɒkər/)
gymnastics	n	/dʒɪm'næstɪks/
hockey	n	/'hɒki/
karate	n	/kə'rɑːti/
horse-riding	n	/'hɔːs raɪdɪŋ/ (AmE /'hɔːrs raɪdɪŋ/)
running	n	/'rʌnɪŋ/
sailing	n	/'seɪlɪŋ/
swimming	n	/'swɪmɪŋ/
skiing	n	/'skiːɪŋ/
skateboarding	n	/'skeɪtbɔːdɪŋ/ (AmE /'skeɪtbɔːrdɪŋ/)
snowboarding	n	/'snəʊbɔːdɪŋ/ (AmE /'snəʊbɔːrdɪŋ/)
surfing	n	/'sɜːfɪŋ/ (AmE /'sɜːrfɪŋ/)
tennis	n	/'tenɪs/
volleyball	n	/'vɒlibɔːl/

Sports and health words

beginner	n	/bɪ'gɪnə(r)/
club	n	/klʌb/
dangerous	adj	/'deɪndʒərəs/
fast food	n	/fɑːst 'fuːd/
fit	adj	/fɪt/
healthy	adj	/'helθi/
lose weight	v	/luːz 'weɪt/
race	n	/reɪs/
team	n	/tiːm/

Unit 9

Animals

bear	n	/beə(r)/
camel	n	/'kæməl/
cat	n	/kæt/
cow	n	/kaʊ/
crocodile	n	/'krɒkədaɪl/
dog	n	/dɒg/
elephant	n	/'elɪfənt/
frog	n	/frɒg/
horse	n	/hɔːs/ (AmE /hɔːrs/)
lion	n	/'laɪən/
monkey	n	/'mʌŋki/
parrot	n	/'pærət/
sheep	n	/ʃiːp/
tiger	n	/'taɪgə(r)/
chicken	n	/'tʃɪkɪn/
fish	n	/fɪʃ/
mouse	n	/maʊs/

Animal words

farm	n	/fɑːm/ (AmE /fɑːrm/)
pet	n	/pet/
wool	n	/wʊl/
zoo	n	/zuː/

Adjectives

beautiful	adj	/'bjuːtɪfl/
big	adj	/bɪg/
dangerous	adj	/'deɪndʒərəs/
dirty	adj	/'dɜːti/ (AmE /'dɜːrti/)
fast	adj	/fɑːst/ (AmE /fæst/)
friendly	adj	/'frendli/
good	adj	/gʊd/
heavy	adj	/'hevi/
intelligent	adj	/ɪn'telɪdʒənt/
noisy	adj	/'nɔɪzi/
slow	adj	/sləʊ/
pretty	adj	/'prɪti/
strong	adj	/strɒŋ/
thirsty	adj	/'θɜːsti/ (AmE /'θɜːrsti/)
ugly	adj	/'ʌgli/

Nature

beach	n	/biːtʃ/
field	n	/fiːld/
flower	n	/'flaʊə(r)/
forest	n	/'fɒrɪst/
grass	n	/grɑːs/ (AmE /græs/)
hill	n	/hɪl/
island	n	/'aɪlənd/
lake	n	/leɪk/
mountain	n	/'maʊntɪn/
plant	n	/plɑːnt/ (AmE /plænt/)
sea	n	/siː/
tree	n	/triː/

Weather

cloudy	adj	/'klaʊdi/
cold	adj	/kəʊld/
dry	adj	/draɪ/
foggy	adj	/'fɒgi/
hot	adj	/hɒt/
ice	n	/aɪs/
rain	v	/reɪn/
snow	v	/snəʊ/
sun	n	/sʌn/
sunny	adj	/'sʌni/
thunderstorm	n	/'θʌndəstɔːm/ (AmE /'θʌndərstɔːm/)
warm	adj	/wɔːm/ (AmE /wɔːrm/)
wind	n	/wɪnd/

Seasons

spring	n	/sprɪŋ/
summer	n	/'sʌmə(r)/
autumn (AmE fall)	n	/'ɔːtəm/ (AmE /fɔːl/)
winter	n	/'wɪntə(r)/
season	n	/'siːzən/

Unit 10

Holidays

guide book	n	/'gaɪd bʊk/
holiday (AmE vacation)	n	/'hɒlɪdeɪ/ (AmE /veɪ'keɪʃn/)
hotel	n	/həʊ'tel/
journey	n	/'dʒɜːni/ (AmE /'dʒɜːrni/)
luggage (AmE baggage)	n	/'lʌgɪdʒ/ (AmE /'bægɪdʒ/)
map	n	/mæp/
postcard	n	/'pəʊstkɑːd/ (AmE /'pəʊstkɑːrd/)
suitcase	n	/'suːtkeɪs/
ticket	n	/'tɪkɪt/
tour guide	n	/'tʊə(r) gaɪd/

tourist information office	n	/'tʊərɪst ɪnfə'meɪʃn ɒfis/ (AmE /'tʊərɪst ɪnfər'meɪʃn ɒfis/)
travel agent	n	/'trævl eɪdʒənt/

Holiday verbs

book	v	/bʊk/
carry	v	/'kæri/
collect	v	/kə'lekt/
pack	v	/pæk/
pay	v	/peɪ/
plan	v	/plæn/
read	v	/riːd/
send	v	/send/
stay	v	/steɪ/
visit	v	/'vɪzɪt/

Transport

aeroplane (AmE airplane)	n	/'eərəpleɪn/ (AmE /'eərpleɪn/)
bicycle	n	/'baɪsɪkl/
boat	n	/bəʊt/
bus	n	/bʌs/
car	n	/kɑː(r)/
coach (AmE bus)	n	/kəʊtʃ/ (AmE /bʌs/)
helicopter	n	/'helɪkɒptə(r)/
motorbike	n	/'məʊtəbaɪk/
parking space	n	/'pɑːkɪŋ speɪs/ (AmE /'pɑːrkɪŋ speɪs/)
plane	n	/pleɪn/
taxi (AmE cab)	n	/'tæksi/ (AmE /kæb/)
train	n	/treɪn/
tram	n	/træm/
underground (AmE subway)	n	/'ʌndəgraʊnd/ (AmE /'sʌbweɪ/)

Transport verbs

catch	v	/kætʃ/
drive	v	/draɪv/
fly	v	/flaɪ/
get in	v	/get 'ɪn/
get off	v	/get 'ɒf/
get on	v	/get 'ɒn/
get out of	v	/get 'aʊt əv/
miss	v	/mɪs/
park	v	/pɑːk/ (AmE /pɑːrk/)
ride	v	/raɪd/
sail	v	/seɪl/
take	v	/teɪk/
travel	v	/'trævl/

Unit 11

Buildings

apartment building	n	/ə'pɑːtmənt bɪldɪŋ/ (AmE /ə'pɑːrtmənt bɪldɪŋ/)
bank	n	/bæŋk/
bridge	n	/brɪdʒ/
castle	n	/'kɑːsl/ (AmE /'kæsl/)
church	n	/tʃɜːtʃ/ (AmE /tʃɜːrtʃ/)
cinema (AmE movie theater)	n	/'sɪnəmə/ (AmE /'muːvi θɪətər/)
factory	n	/'fæktri/
hospital	n	/'hɒspɪtl/
library	n	/'laɪbri/
museum	n	/mjuː'ziːəm/
office building	n	/'ɒfɪs bɪldɪŋ/
post office	n	/'pəʊst ɒfɪs/
railway station (AmE railroad station)	n	/'reɪlweɪ steɪʃn/ (AmE /'reɪlrəʊd steɪʃn/)

stadium	n	/'steɪdiəm/
ruin	n	/'ruːɪn/
skatepark	n	/'skeɪtpɑːk/ (AmE /'skeɪtpɑːrk/)
sports centre (AmE sports center)	n	/'spɔːts sentə(r)/ (AmE /'spɔːrts sentər/)
swimming pool	n	/'swɪmɪŋ puːl/
theatre (AmE theater)	n	/'θɪətə(r)/
university	n	/juːnɪ'vɜːsəti/ (AmE /juːnɪ'vɜːrsəti/)

Places in town

crossroads	n	/'krɒsrəʊdz/
market place	n	/'mɑːkɪt pleɪs/ (AmE /'mɑːrkɪt pleɪs/)
roundabout (AmE traffic circle)	n	/'raʊndəbaʊt/ (AmE /'træfɪk sɜːrkl/)
traffic lights	n	/'træfɪk laɪts/

Directions

behind	prep	/bɪ'haɪnd/
between	prep	/bɪ'twiːn/
in front of	prep	/ɪn 'frʌnt əv/
next to	prep	/'nekst tu/
opposite	prep	/'ɒpəsɪt/
past	prep	/pɑːst/ (AmE /pæst/)
turn left	v	/tɜːn 'left/ (AmE /tɜːrn 'left/)
turn right	v	/tɜːn 'raɪt/ (AmE /tɜːrn 'raɪt/)
go straight on	v	/gəʊ 'streɪt ɒn/

Unit 12

Technology

computer	n	/kəm'pjuːtə(r)/
email	n	/'iːmeɪl/
games console	n	/'geɪmz kɒnsəʊl/
internet	n	/'ɪntənet/ (AmE /'ɪntərnet/)
keyboard	n	/'kiːbɔːd/ (AmE /'kiːbɔːrd/)
laptop	n	/'læptɒp/
mobile phone (AmE cell phone)	n	/məʊbaɪl 'fəʊn/ (AmE /'selfəʊn/)
MP3 player	n	/em piː 'θriː pleɪə(r)/
online	adv	/ɒn'laɪn/
radio	n	/'reɪdiəʊ/
screen	n	/skriːn/
technology	n	/tek'nɒlədʒi/
television	n	/telɪ'vɪʒn/
text message	n	/'tekst mesɪdʒ/
website	n	/'websaɪt/

Technology verbs

chat	v	/'tʃæt/
record	v	/rɪ'kɔːd/ (AmE /rɪ'kɔːrd/)
send	v	/send/
surf	v	/sɜːf/ (AmE /sɜːrf/)
type	v	/taɪp/
visit	v	/'vɪzɪt/

Books and reading

advertisement	n	/əd'vɜːtɪsmənt/ (AmE /əd'vɜːrtɪsmənt/)
article	n	/'ɑːtɪkl/ (AmE /'ɑːrtɪkl/)
cartoon	n	/kɑː'tuːn/ (AmE /kɑːr'tuːn/)
comic	n	/'kɒmɪk/
crossword	n	/'krɒswɜːd/ (AmE /'krɒswɜːrd/)
dictionary	n	/'dɪkʃənri/
magazine	n	/mægə'ziːn/ (AmE /'mægəziːn/)
newspaper	n	/'njuːzpeɪpə(r)/
novel	n	/'nɒvl/
photograph	n	/'fəʊtəgrɑːf/ (AmE /'fəʊtəgræf/)
weather report	n	/'weðə rɪpɔːt/ (AmE /'weðər rɪpɔːrt/)

CAMBRIDGE UNIVERSITY PRESS
www.cambridge.org/elt

RICHMOND PUBLISHING
www.richmondelt.com

© Richmond Publishing 2010
(KET for Schools *Direct* was originally published by
Richmond Publishing as *Target KET for Schools*
© Richmond Publishing 2009)

Printed in Hong Kong

ISBN 978-0-521-16717-8 Student's Book with CD-ROM
ISBN 978-0-521-16718-5 Workbook without answers
ISBN 978-0-521-16719-2 Workbook with answers
ISBN 978-0521-16720-8 Teacher's Book with Class Audio CD
ISBN 978-0521-16721-5 Student's Pack (*Student's Book with CD-ROM and Workbook without answers*)

Acknowledgements:

Publisher: Deborah Tricker
Commissioning Editor: Matthew Duffy
Development Editor: Graham Skerritt
Proofreader: Soo Hamilton
Design and Layout: Rob Briggs, Dave Kuzmicki
Cover Design: Georgie French
Photo Research: Magdalena Mayo
Audio Production: Paul Ruben Productions, Inc. NYC
Legal consulting and copyright clearance: Ruz Legal,
Spain

Publisher acknowledgements:
The publishers would like to thank the following
reviewers for their valuable feedback which has made
this project possible.

Elizabeth Beck (Italy), Gertrude Baxter (Universad
Tecnologica de la Mixteca, Mexico), Claudia Bonilla
Cassani (Colegio del Tepeyac, Mexico), Maria
Consuelo Velasco (Colombia), Karen Dyer (Madrid,
Spain), Melissa Ferrin (Universad Tecnologica de
la Mixteca, Mexico), Angieszka Gugnacka-Cook
(ELC Łódź, Poland), Andrea Harries (The English
Company, Colombia), Analía Kandel (Argentina),
Gabby Maguire (International House Barcelona, Spain),
Roberta Natalini (Intuition Languages-IH, UK), Laura
Renart (ISP Dr Sáenz, Universad Virtual de Quilmes,
Argentina), Agnieszka Tyszkiewicz-Zora (ELC Łódź,
Poland)

The publishers would also like to thank all those who
have given their kind permission to reproduce or adapt
material for this book.

Texts:
p 46 "Close the door we're trying to sleep"
© 2008 MailOnline. All rights reserved

p 57 "13yo girl is nu wrld txt msgng champion"
© 2007 Telegraph.co.uk. All rights reserved

Illustrations:
Charlene Chua, William Donohoe, Scott Garrett,
Matt Johnstone, Terry Wong

Photographs:
J. Jaime; J. M.ª Escudero/Instituto Municipal de
Deportes de Madrid; J. V. Resino; KAIBIDE DE CARLOS
FOTÓGRAFOS; Krauel; Prats i Camps; S. Enríquez;
A. G. E. FOTOSTOCK/Walter Bibikow, TOPIC PHOTO
AGENCY IN, SuperStock, Corbis, Banana Stock,
Roderick Chen; ABB FOTÓGRAFOS; ACI AGENCIA
DE FOTOGRAFÍA/Alamy Images, Denkou Images;
COMSTOCK; CORDON PRESS/CORBIS/Neal Preston,
Gene Blevins; DIGITALVISION; EFE; FOTONONSTOP;
GETTY IMAGES SALES SPAIN/Gareth Davies,
Chris Jackson, Brian Hendler, Julie Fisher, Jason
Kempin, Hola Images, Dan Kitwood, Louise Wilson,
AFP, Photodisc/David De Lossy, FilmMagic/Jason
Merritt, Michael S. Yamashita, Taxi/Britt Erlanson,
Iconica/Peter Cade, Dorling Kindersley, AFP/Geoff
Caddick, Stone/Ed Freeman, Taxi/James Ross, Shaun
Botterill, Photodisc/Nina Frenkel, Hulton Archive,
Digital Vision, WireImage/Ferdaus Shamim, UpperCut
Images/Susan Wides, Scott Wintrow; HIGHRES PRESS
STOCK/AbleStock.com; ISTOCKPHOTO; JOHN FOXX
IMAGES; LONDON MEDIA PRESS; PHOTODISC; STOCK
PHOTOS/Blend Images; Newspix/Rex Features; wishlist
images; SERIDEC PHOTOIMAGENES CD/DigitalVision;
TUMBLEWEED TINY HOUSE COMPANY;
ARCHIVO SANTILLANA